The Journal of Andrew Fuller Studies

Published in the United States of America by
by The Andrew Fuller Center for Baptist Studies
The Southern Baptist Theological Seminary
2825 Lexington Road
Louisville, Kentucky 40280

© The Andrew Fuller Center for Baptist Studies 2023

All rights reserved. No part of this publication may be reproduced, stored in a retrieval system, or transmitted, in any form or by any means, without the prior permission in writing of The Andrew Fuller Center for Baptist Studies, or as expressly permitted by law, by license, or under terms agreed with the appropriate reproduction rights organization.

ISBN 978-1-77484-112-9

Printed by H&E Publishing, Peterborough, Ontario, Canada

The Journal of Andrew Fuller Studies

The *Journal of Andrew Fuller Studies* is an open access, double-blind peer-reviewed, scholarly journal published online biannually in February and September by the Andrew Fuller Center for Baptist Studies (under the auspices of The Southern Baptist Theological Seminary). The publication language of the journal is English. Articles that deal with the life, ministry, and thought of the Baptist pastor-theologian Andrew Fuller are very welcome, as well as essays on his friends, his Particular Baptist community in the long eighteenth century (1680s–1830s), and the global impact of his thought, known as "Fullerism."

Articles and book reviews are to follow generally the style of Kate L. Turabian, *A Manual for Writers of Research Papers, Theses, and Dissertations*, 9th ed. (Chicago: University of Chicago Press, 2018). They may be submitted in British, American, Australian, New Zealand, or Canadian English. Articles should be between 5,000 and 8,000 words, excluding footnotes. Articles are to be sent to the Editor and book reviews to the Book Review Editors.

Editor:
Michael A G Haykin, ThD, FRHistS
Chair & Professor of Church History
& Director, The Andrew Fuller Center for Baptist Studies
The Southern Baptist Theological Seminary, Louisville, Kentucky
mhaykin@sbts.edu

Associate editor:
Baiyu Andrew Song, PhD cand.
Assistant Professor of General Education Studies
Heritage College and Seminary
Cambridge, Ontario
bsong@heritagecs.edu

Design editor:
Dustin W. Benge, PhD
Associate Professor of Biblical Spirituality and Historical Theology
& Vice President of Communications
The Southern Baptist Theological Seminary, Louisville, Kentucky

Book review editor:
Caleb Anthony Neel, PhD cand.
The Southern Baptist Theological Seminary, Louisville, Kentucky
cneel914@students.sbts.edu

Editorial board:
Cindy Aalders, DPhil
Director of the John Richard Allison Library
& Assistant Professor of the History of Christianity
Regent College, Vancouver

Dustin Benge, PhD
Associate Professor of Biblical Spirituality and Historical Theology
& Vice President of Communications
The Southern Baptist Theological Seminary
Louisville, Kentucky

Dustin B. Bruce, PhD
Dean & Assistant Professor of Christian Theology and Church History
Boyce College
Louisville, Kentucky

Chris W. Crocker, PhD
Pastor, Markdale Baptist Church, ON
& Associate Professor of Church History
Toronto Baptist Seminary
Toronto, Ontario

Chris Chun, PhD
Professor of Church History & Director of the Jonathan Edwards Center
Gateway Seminary
Ontario, California

Jenny-Lyn de Klerk, PhD
Editor, Book Division
Crossway
Wheaton, Illinois

Jason G. Duesing, PhD
Provost & Professor of Historical Theology
Midwestern Baptist Theological Seminary
Kansas City, Missouri

Nathan A. Finn, PhD
Provost & Dean of the University Faculty
North Greenville University
Tigerville, South Carolina

C. Ryan Griffith, PhD
Pastor, Cities Church
St. Paul, Minnesota

Peter J. Morden, PhD
Senior Pastor/Team Leader, Cornerstone Baptist Church
Leeds, England
& Distinguished Visiting Scholar
Spurgeon's College
London, England

Adriaan C. Neele, PhD
Director, Doctoral Program & Professor of Historical Theology
Puritan Reformed Theological Seminary
Grand Rapids, Michigan
& Research Scholar
Yale University, Jonathan Edwards Center
New Haven, Connecticut

Robert Strivens, PhD
Pastor, Bradford on Avon Baptist Church (UK)
& Lecturer in Church History
London Seminary
London, England

Tom Nettles, PhD
Senior Professor of Historical Theology
The Southern Baptist Theological Seminary
Louisville, Kentucky

Blair Waddell, PhD
Pastor, Providence Baptist Church
Huntsville, Alabama

Contents

The Journal of Andrew Fuller Studies
No. 6, February 2023

Editorial Michael A.G. Haykin	9
Articles Andrew Fuller's tour of Ireland, June 1804 Gary Brady	11
The excellent Mr. Burls: First London Member of the Committee and Third Treasurer of the Baptist Missionary Society; First Treasurer of the Irish Baptist Society Ernest A. Payne	23
Hannah Marshman: A founding missionary of the Serampore Mission Sydney Dixon	33
"I have a much larger room to sleep in, and good closets for my books": A study of Joseph Kinghorn's library catalogue Baiyu Andrew Song	57
Texts & documents Jane Potter (c. 1761–1808) of Bath ed. Courtney Bachert	73
"Dr. M will go down": Joseph Kinghorn (1766–1832) on two Baptist controversies ed. Baiyu Andrew Song	79
Book reviews	89

Editorial

Michael A.G. Haykin

Michael A.G. Haykin is Chair and Professor of Church History and Director, The Andrew Fuller Center for Baptist Studies at The Southern Baptist Theological Seminary, Louisville, Kentucky.

By naming Andrew Fuller in the title of this journal, we are recognizing the vital role that biography needs to play in the telling of the story of the church. It is all too easy to think that impersonal factors, such as ideas and ideologies or geography and cultural movements, should occupy the central role in the history of Christianity. But it is people, gripped by ideas and filtering them through their own personal make-up and historical and cultural context, whom God uses to advance his church.

In this issue we have three essays that focus on three important figures in Baptist life in the long eighteenth century. Gary Brady looks at Andrew Fuller's sole visit to Ireland, which took place in 1804. This small period from Fuller's life well reveals his missionary passion and longing for spiritual maturity among the churches of Christ. The library of Fuller's friend, the scholarly Joseph Kinghorn, is the subject of an essay by Baiyu Andrew Song, who displays the remarkable erudition of this Baptist minister. The final essay, by missionary Sydney Dixon, looks at a past missionary, namely Hannah Marshman, whom Dixon's essay reveals to have been a central figure, albeit a forgotten one, in the early years of the Serampore Mission.

Of course, a biographical approach to church history, as exemplified in these three essays, does not remove the need to explore the role that, for instance, ideas and culture, geography and politics play in the life of the church. Nonetheless, it is a great reminder of the importance of people to God and to the gospel, and that should be important to historical scholarship.

Andrew Fuller's tour of Ireland, June 1804

Gary Brady

Gary Brady, ThM, has been the pastor of Childs Hill Baptist Church, London, since 1983.

In his lifetime, the Baptist preacher and theologian Andrew Fuller (1754–1815) made just one brief trip to Ireland. After 1792, it was his pattern to travel extensively across the British Isles from his base in Kettering in connection with the missionary society that supported William Carey (1761–1834) and his fellow workers in India, known originally as "The Particular Baptist Society for the Propagation of the Gospel Amongst the Heathen." Fuller would spend as much as three months a year away from his family and flock during this period. His travels took him to visit churches in all parts of England, five times to Scotland and once to Wales in 1812, as well as to Ireland in 1804.[1]

At that time, the island of Ireland was part of the United Kingdom. Crawford Gribben points out that at the time, its population was much larger than today and was divided by extremes of wealth and poverty, as well as language and religion.[2] The language divide was between English and Gaelic speakers. The rich were generally associated with the established Church of Ireland, and the poor with Roman Catholicism. Anglicanism dominated the whole island, but Presbyterianism was common in the northeast counties, where Scots had settled early in the seventeenth century and were very influential. There were other dissenters but no sense of a common Protestant cause. Anglicanism was resented for the way, for example, it routinely invalidated Presbyterian marriages and prevented Catholics from owning land, injustices both real and felt.

---

[1] The years that Fuller visited Scotland were 1799, 1802, 1805, 1808, and 1813.

[2] Crawford Gribben, *The Revival of Particular Baptist Life in Ireland 1780–1840*, 2nd ed. (Louisville, KY: Andrew Fuller Centre for Baptist Studies, 2018), 1.

Baptist witness in Dublin goes back to 1653, to the Cromwellian era, when, through the ministry of an Englishman, Thomas Patient (d. 1666), the first Particular Baptist meeting house was built in Swift's Alley, Dublin.[3] At first, Patient's congregation grew rapidly. By 1725 there were 150–200 members and a new meeting house was erected in the 1730s. However, by the end of the eighteenth century, membership had dwindled to forty or less.[4] There were as many as ten Baptist congregations in Ireland at one point. However, by the end of the eighteenth century, only six survived and were in danger of becoming extinct. Gribben identifies at least four factors in the decline. First, dependence on an occupying military force—military protection was lost after the Cromwellian administration's collapse. Second, a loss of economic strength when, at the Restoration, Baptist landowners who remained in Ireland lost significant portions of their estates. Third, many wealthy Baptists were gripped by worldliness. Their wealth increased, and their commitment to the Baptist community tended to wane. Fourth, a lack of doctrinal clarity. As early as 1725, it is claimed, the Baptist churches had lost their earlier doctrinal uniformity, and many tended to become isolated.[5]

Pearce's visit in 1796

Fuller was familiar with the situation in Ireland to some extent. In 1800, when Fuller published the biography of Samuel Pearce (1766-1799), he included the latter's six-week trip to Ireland, by the invitation of the General Evangelical Society, in June and July 1796.[6] Pearce left his Birmingham home at 8 am on May 31 and, passing through North Wales, took ship from Holyhead to Dublin, arriving on the afternoon of Saturday, June 4. He stayed with a wealthy Presbyterian elder, Henry Hutton (1755-1808). Hutton had been high sheriff of Dublin in 1792 and later the Lord Mayor. He was a member of the Presbyterian congregation known as the Scots Church that met at Mary's Abbey, pastored by Benjamin McDowell (1739-1824), who was the man behind the invitation to Pearce.[7] Pearce preached for McDowell's congregation several times during

---

[3] B.R. White, "Thomas Patient in England and Ireland," *Irish Baptist Historical Society Journal* 2 (1969-1970): 41.

[4] Joshua Thompson, "Baptists in Ireland 1792–1922: A Dimension of Protestant Dissent" (DPhil Thesis, Regent's Park College, University of Oxford, 1988), 9.

[5] See Gribben, *Revival of Particular Baptist Life in Ireland*, 12–13.

[6] Michael A.G. Haykin, ed., *Memoirs of Samuel Pearce*, Complete Works of Andrew Fuller, Volume 4 (Berlin: De Gruyter, 2017). The General Evangelical Society was formed in 1787 by Selina Hastings, Countess of Huntingdon's (1707–1791) connexion preachers. Pearce was not the first Baptist to be invited, John Rippon (1751–1836) and others had also received invitation.

[7] McDowell was born in New Jersey and trained for the ministry at Princeton and Glasgow. He was

his stay. He also preached for an independent church in Plunkett Street, where he also heard the radical Presbyterian Sinclare Kelburn (1754–1802), and other congregations in the city.[8]

Pearce's impressions of the Swift's Alley congregation were none too positive. In a letter written to his close friend Carey in August 1796, the month after he returned to England, he wrote: "When I came to Dublin they had no meeting of any kind for religious purposes … Indeed they were so dead to piety that, tho' of their own denomination, I saw & knew less of them than of every other professors in the place."[9] Nevertheless, some in the congregation lapped up Pearce's preaching, as a Dublin deacon wrote to a friend: "We have had a Jubilee for weeks. That blessed man of God, Samuel Pearce, has preached amongst us with great sweetness and much power."[10]

Irish Rebellion and Fuller's Trip

Between the visits of Pearce and Fuller, Ireland experienced the Irish Rebellion of 1798, a major uprising against English rule in Ireland, organised by the Society of United Irishmen—a republican revolutionary group influenced by the American and French Revolutions. Originally formed by Presbyterian radicals, angry at being shut out of power by the Anglican establishment, it was soon supported by many from the majority Catholic population. Thousands of rebels died when the rebellion was quickly suppressed. Even when Fuller was in Ireland, he would perhaps have been aware of some continuing guerrilla warfare.[11]

---

called to Dublin in 1778. Upon his arrival, church membership was no more than half a dozen families. During his pastorate, the congregation grew remarkably and reached to two thousand.

[8] On Kelburn, see Douglas Armstrong, *Rev. Sinclare Kelburn, 1754–1802 Preacher, Pastor, Patriot* (Belfast: Presbyterian Historical Society of Ireland, 2001).

Pearce told Rippon that there were four Presbyterian congregations in Dublin. Two were orthodox, a small one and a large one, under McDowell's charge. Pearce also knew of a Countess of Huntingdon connexion society there: "the only one in the kingdom, perhaps, except at Sligo, where there is another." Not large, Pearce feared it was declining. He knew of six Baptist churches but no Congregationalists. See Haykin, ed., *Memoirs of Samuel Pearce*, 85.

[9] Samuel Pearce to William Carey, August 1796, Pearce Family Letters, Samuel Pearce Carey Collection (Angus Library, Regent's Park College, Oxford).

[10] In a letter to a close friend in London, Pearce acknowledged: "Never have I been more deeply taught my own nothingness, never has the power of God more evidently rested upon me. The harvest here is great indeed; and the Lord of the harvest has enabled me to labour in it with delight" (Haykin, ed., *Memoir of Rev. Samuel Pearce*, 79).

[11] Fuller wrote to Carey at the time: "We have had an awful struggle in Ireland. 40,000 United Irishmen it appears have been slain!" (Andrew Fuller, Letter to William Carey, August 22, 1798, typescript in Andrew Fuller Letters 4/5/1, 4/5/2 [Angus Library, Regent's Park College, Oxford]).

It was at the beginning of June 1804 that Fuller made his own trip to Ireland. We do not have his itinerary as we do with his later trip to Wales, but we have material recounting his impressions and some of his private conversations with those on the ground. His purpose was

> not only to receive pecuniary aid for the mission from the wealthy professors of religion in Dublin, but to confirm the important services rendered to the churches of that city and neighbourhood by … Pearce, and establish a connexion which, while it tended to remove from those churches the frigid influence of Sandemanianism, might prove mutually beneficial to the spiritual interests of both countries.[12]

There is no evidence that Fuller ventured out of Dublin. His purpose, according to his biographer John Webster Morris (1763–1836), was "to visit the Baptist churches in that part of the kingdom, and collect for the mission."[13] It was not an ideal period to be away as two of his children were dangerously ill at the time, a four-year-old at home and another in his early twenties, away from home.[14] Nevertheless, Fuller "left home under great depression, and took an

---

[12] Andrew Gunton Fuller, "Memoir" in *The Complete Works of the Rev. Andrew Fuller*, ed. Joseph Belcher (Reprint, Harrisonburg, VA: Sprinkle, 1988), 1:82. In 1810, Fuller wrote and published *Strictures on Sandemanianism* (see Nathan A. Finn, ed., *Apologetic Works 5 Strictures on Sandemanianism*, Works of Andrew Fuller 9 [Berlin: De Gruyter, 2016]). About this work, Ian H. Clary comments, "it is likely that [Fuller's] experiences with it in Ireland contributed to his reasons for writing" (Clary, "'Melting the ice of a long winter': Revival and Irish Dissent," in *Pentecostal Outpourings: Revival and the Reformed Tradition*, eds. Robert Davis Smart, Michael A.G. Haykin, and Ian Hugh Clary (Grand Rapids, MI: Reformation Heritage Books, 2015), 48.

Sandemanians, originally Glasites, began around 1730 in Scotland, when Church of Scotland minister John Glas (1695–1773) rejected the idea of a state church as being non-New Testament. He taught that the Christian church is essentially spiritual and cannot be upheld by political or secular means. Expelled from the Church of Scotland, he established his own church, first in Dundee, then Perth. His son-in-law Robert Sandeman (1718–1771) succeeded him as leader of the sect. Sandemanians were marked by a predominantly intellectualist view of faith and became known for their cardinal theological tenet that saving faith is "bare belief of the bare truth." They also had a restorationist approach to church life, attempting to conform to primitive Christianity as they understood it. Each congregation had a plural eldership, chosen independently of education or occupation. The Lord's Supper was observed weekly, and each Sunday at noon a feast was held, attended by all members. Foot washing and the holy kiss were also practiced. They believed accumulation of wealth was unbiblical and improper. They were never numerous and they gradually declined. However, their churches in Scotland, England and America were influential.

[13] J.W. Morris, *Memoirs of the Life and Writings of the Rev. Andrew Fuller* (Boston, 1830), 100.

[14] Fuller married twice. After the death of his first wife, Sarah Gardiner (1756–1792), Fuller married Ann Coles (d. 1825) in late 1794, a daughter of Baptist pastor William Coles (1735–1809) of Ampthill, who ministered at Maulden, Bedfordshire. With Sarah, Fuller had 11 children, eight of whom survived to adulthood. With Ann, he had another six, and three died in infancy. See Matthew Haste, "Marriage and Family in the Life of Andrew Fuller," *Southern Baptist Journal of Theology* 17.1 (2013): 28–34; Michael A.G. Haykin,

affectionate leave of his people."[15] As Gribben observes, Fuller's visit contrasted entirely with that of Pearce. Fuller found much to discourage, as "in total contrast to the experience of Pearce, Fuller's visit was not to be a triumphant success."[16] Nevertheless, he was resolute about undertaking the journey. Arriving in Dublin, he found himself in a new situation and was struck by the abundance of poverty and superstition, not seen to the same degree in England.[17] On the first Sunday, he preached in the morning at Swift's Alley. Fuller was somewhat disappointed to see only a few middle-class people, not more than forty or fifty, scattered about in a place of worship that could hold four hundred people. He also preached for McDowell, as Pearce had done. In the afternoon, less than two hundred people gathered in a place that could hold nearly two thousand; in the evening, there were only about forty more. These congregations were very different from what he had seen in Scotland two years before. He said in a letter that they appeared "like the heads at Temple Bar, without bodies."[18] Afterwards, his hearers increased to between fifteen hundred and two thousand.

Fuller noted that the congregations were all Protestants, as scarcely any Catholic would attend. Even Roman Catholics who were servants in Protestant families would seldom attend family worship. All the Protestant denominations in England were present in Ireland. However, there was a significant lack of spiritual vibrance and a lamentable indifference toward the fundamental truths of the gospel everywhere in Ireland. Worse, Fuller noticed that the laxity was not only in doctrines but also morality, as he was surprised to hear people "pleading for a harmless game of cards, for the innocence of the stage, and the virtue of theatrical performers."[19] For these reasons, Fuller could not conscien-

The Armies of the Lamb: The Spirituality of Andrew Fuller (Dundas, ON: Joshua Press, 2001), 283–288.

[15] In a letter written at the time, at the close of the Sabbath, Fuller wrote: "I have baptized five persons to day, and preached my farewell sermon to the church, from John xvii. 21. I considered, (1) The object prayed for—union—'that they all may be one.' (2) The model of it—the union between the Father and the Son, or between the Lawgiver and the Saviour, in the work of human redemption—'as thou Father art in me, and I in thee.' (3) Its influence on mankind—that the world may believe that thou hast sent me" (Morris, *Memoirs*, 119).

[16] For Gribben, Fuller's engineering of the split of the principal Dublin Baptist congregation "was certainly not the revival that Pearce appeared to have experienced and which Fuller might have expected" (Gribben, *Revival of Particular Baptist Life*, 11).

[17] Fuller was aware of Irish poverty. While travelling by coach, Fuller met with some Irish reapers returning home. They complained that they had been paid chiefly in one pound country notes, which they would only be able to exchange in Dublin with a considerable loss, if at all. Fuller had an unusual amount of cash in guineas and exchanged them for these notes. These poor men were very grateful. See Andrew Gunton Fuller, *Andrew Fuller* (London: Hodder and Stoughton, 1882), 82.

[18] This suggests that the church was fitted with the high box pews that were common at the time.

[19] Morris, *Memoirs*, 100.

tiously comply and declined the invitation to administer the Lord's Supper in a Baptist chapel.

Dr. Walker

During his stay in Dublin, Fuller was visited by John Walker (c.1767–1838), who was "one of the most promising [or hopeful] of Pearce's contacts" in 1796.[20] By the time Fuller met him, Walker embraced Sandemanianism and had considerable influence in the city. When Walker said of a preacher, "he preaches the gospel," Fuller realised it simply meant the man was thinking of embracing Sandemanianism. Similarly, when he said that Baptist and Moravian ministers were not preaching the gospel, he meant that they were not about to become Sandemanians. "I found him, like most of the sect," observed Fuller, "calm, acute, versed in the Scriptures, but void of feeling. He reminded me of Dr. Byrom's lines: ''Tis Athens' owl, and not Mount Zion's dove,/The bird of learning, not the bird of love.'"[21] Fuller wrote in a letter that he heard that one of this group prayed in public: "Lord, give me head-knowledge; the rest I leave to thee."[22]

Walker told Fuller his complaints about some Calvinists, who were "as far from the truth as Arminians."[23] In response, Fuller asked Walker to clarify who was he referring to and in what way they were worse. For Walker, the Calvinists he referred to were "those who hold with qualifications as necessary to warrant a sinner's believing."[24] Fuller could not identify any Calvinist who held such beliefs. Though Samuel Stennett (1780–1841), a graduate of Bristol Academy and a minister in Dublin, suggested that these might be the high Calvinists, Fuller told Walker that he "utterly disapproved of" high Calvinism, "though I could not ... condemn all, as graceless, who held it."[25] Fuller's answer surprised Walker. At the same time, it showed to Fuller that Walker and other Sandema-

---

[20] John Walker was ordained in the Church of Ireland and was elected as a fellow of Trinity College, Dublin. As an evangelical, Walker sought to return to apostolic practices and was expelled from his fellowship and clerical order in 1804. He later embraced Sandemanianism. Gribben, *Revival of Particular Baptist Life*, 7, 10.

[21] John Ryland, *The Work of Faith: The Labour of Love, and the Patience of Hope, Illustrated; in the Life and Death of the Rev. Andrew Fuller, Late Pastor of the Baptist Church at Kettering, and Secretary to the Baptist Missionary Society* (London, 1818), 229. The poem came from English poet John Byrom's (1692–1793) "An Answer to Some Enquiries, Concerning the Author's Opinion of a Sermon Preached at— upon the Operations of the Holy Spirit," in *Miscellaneous Poems* (Manchester, 1773), 1:206.

[22] Ryland, *Work of Faith*, 229.

[23] Ryland, *Work of Faith*, 229.

[24] Ryland, *Work of Faith*, 230.

[25] Ryland, *Work of Faith*, 230.

nians could not differentiate pleading for a holy disposition and the notion that holiness gave a warrant to believe. For Fuller, a characteristic of Irish Sandemanianism was that they made a marked separation in public worship between those they reckoned believers and those they reckoned unbelievers. This came down to the seats they were allowed to occupy, as "unbelievers" were not allowed to sit with "believers," nor could public prayer be said in a mixed company. Fuller asked one of the Irish Sandemanians, William Cooper (1776–1848), "whether he would engage in family prayer, if his wife, being present, were in his account an unbeliever? He answered, No: and I find that family worship is nearly, if not wholly neglected among them."[26] Fuller's view was later confirmed to be accurate by an Edinburgh minister, who spent some time among them. This Scottish minister also told Fuller that "Sandemanianism as a system was … the most destructive of pure religion of any thing in any sect; acknowledging at the same time, that very little regard was paid to family worship; that their children were brought up without discipline, and in habits of dissipation."[27] Nevertheless, these Irish Sandemanians were not followed by others in all their practices.

More positive encounters

Fuller met others in Ireland who impressed him. In a letter to William Ward (1769–1823) in 1804, Fuller told his friend, "There is a lovely man among the Moravians in Ireland, and another, Mr. Kelly, the son of a judge, and an Independent. They are doing much good, but the Sandemanians say they do not preach the gospel."[28] In the same letter, Fuller also wrote:

> I can perceive that the galling circumstance to the Irish is, that about a seventh part of the population rule the rest; and hence they are ever meditating some sort of revenge. If Ireland could be considered as insulated from Britain, it would seem right that so great a majority should

---

[26] Morris, *Memoirs*, 101. William Cooper was a minister at Plunkett Street. Originally living in London, he was converted there through Thomas Haweis (1734–1820) and began preaching in many places. He had a special interest in reaching to the Jews. Walker invited him to itinerate in Ireland and he did so more than once, eventually settling permanently in Dublin, from 1802. Much influenced by Walker, Cooper appears to have come to more orthodox views. In 1828, he had a stroke and was unable to preach for the last twenty years of his life. His son William Haweis Cooper (1797–1847) was a minister at Zion and a teacher at the Dublin Academy.

[27] Morris, *Memoirs*, 101.

[28] Fuller, *Andrew Fuller*, 136. The Moravian is identified as John Hartley (d. 1811), who was in Dublin many years and ended his days in Grace Hill, Co Antrim. Mr. Kelley is Thomas Kelly (1769–1855), son of Thomas Kelly (1723–1809), who is best remembered as a hymn writer. He began studying law but entered the church in 1792 only to be thrown out for his evangelical views. He still preached and from 1802 gathered a group known as "Kellyites." He broke with the established church in 1803.

have the rule; but if it be only an integral part of one great empire, the case is quite altered; for if the Catholics could gain the ascendency, there appears to be no doubt but they would persecute, if not massacre the Protestants; and such a state of things would endanger the British empire. If, indeed, they would tolerate the Protestants, in the same manner as the Protestants tolerate them, it would be reasonable that the Catholic population should have the ascendency. But if not, they are like a mob in one of our counties, which, though they may have the great mass of the people on their side, ought not to be suffered to bear rule. Yet I should rejoice to see the Catholics emancipated, and placed on an equal footing with the Protestants, England at the same time keeping up a strong military force to prevent their doing any mischief. I wish at least that the experiment should be tried. If they attempted to abuse their privileges, let them be afterwards curtailed. It has been said by some, that the zeal for Catholic emancipation has nearly subsided; and that if they had their liberty, they would now be friendly. Yet it is a fact, that though when the Dublin Catholics collect for a public charity, they invite Protestants, and they go and give; yet at Protestant charities, the opulent Catholics, when invited in return, will neither go nor give, at least but very rarely.[29]

The return
Having collected about £150 for the mission and preached in various places, Fuller returned home the first week in July to find his family in very difficult circumstances.[30] During his absence his four-year-old had tragically died at home. An older son, the source of his greatest troubles, was dangerously ill and unlikely to recover, away from home. Reflecting on his trip, Fuller wrote to his father-in-law:

> I have enjoyed but little comfort in Ireland. The state of my family at home, the contentions of the Sandemanians at Dublin, the disorders among the Baptists - all together, overwhelmed my spirits. Yet I hope I have derived some profit. The doctrine of the Cross is more sweet to me than ever, and some of my best times in preaching have been from such texts as these; Unto you that believe, he is precious—That they all may be one, as thou Father art in me, and I in thee—He hath sent me to preach the acceptable year of the Lord—He that hath the Son hath life—Now is

---

[29] Morris, *Memoirs*, 102.

[30] Gribben, *Revival of Particular Baptists*, 11. Clary noticed that "it was evidence of the differing theological and economic circumstances of the Dublin churches that £106.15.7½ came from the Presbyterian church at Mary's Abbey." Some £15,000 in today's terms, it was not as much as he had wished (Clary, "Melting the ice of a long winter," 48).

the Son of Man glorified, and God is glorified in him. Oh that for me to live may be Christ! I wish never to preach another sermon but what shall bear some relation to him. I see and feel more and more, that except I eat the flesh and drink the blood of the Son of Man, I have no life in me, either as a Christian or as a minister.[31]

The trip appears to have had some sound effects on the work of the gospel in Ireland. Fuller had tried to bring about a reformation among the Baptists and, failing to achieve this, had assisted in forming a new society founded on better principles. On returning, he drew up a report, as requested, "Remarks on the State of the Baptist Churches in Ireland." In it, Fuller alleged that several members of the church in Swift's Alley, Dublin,

> had disowned some of the most important doctrines of the gospel; such as the Trinity, the atonement, and justification by the imputed righteousness of Christ; that not only the church of which they were members refused to exclude them, but that a motion for that purpose was rejected by their general Association; and that on this ground a considerable part of the church in Swift's Alley separated, and in August, 1804, formed themselves into a new church.[32]

This Report was read and approved at a meeting of Baptist ministers in London and was afterwards adopted by a committee of the Baptist Missionary Society and ordered to be printed. When the Irish churches published their circular letter in 1805, they admitted in reply, that they were greatly deficient, both in regard to vital godliness and church discipline and they deeply lamented that it was so. At the same time, they made a declaration of their religious views in order to vindicate themselves in light of the charges made in Fuller's remarks. They complained that they had been much misunderstood and misrepresented. Their statement was later published in the *Theological and Biblical Magazine*.[33]

Fuller took the opportunity to counterattack by means of the same organ. He wrote:

> In this Vindication it is observable, (1) That the declaration of their re-

---

[31] Fuller, "Memoir," 1:83.

[32] Morris, *Memoirs*, 103.

[33] *The Theological and Biblical Magazine* was edited by J.W. Morris, who pastored the congregations at Clipstone, Northamptonshire, and Dunstable, Bedfordshire. He also worked a printer for the BMS and others.

ligious sentiments' makes no mention of an atonement, or of imputed righteousness. (2) That the article on the Trinity is worded in so cautious a manner, as to be capable of being understood of a modal or Swedenborgian trinity. (3) That if this declaration of their sentiments be not intended to leave room for those who disown three divine Persons in the Godhead, the vicarious sacrifice of Christ, and justification by his righteousness imputed; and if, while they warn their members against conformity to the world, they do not mean to retain such characters among them as plead for the innocence of the theatre and the card table; but are in good earnest resolved to disown them, the breach at Swift's Alley would at once be healed. For those who have withdrawn, have declared in their letter to the church "that if at any future time the church should restore that purity of communion which is essential to a Christian society, they shall be ready to join heart and hand with them." But (4) If this declaration of their sentiments be intended to leave room for such characters, the whole is a mere subterfuge; and instead of proving the *Remarks* erroneous, or the separation schismatical, it abundantly justifies both the one and the other.[34]

John Ryland (1753–1825) later wrote, "Mr. F. certainly acted a very conscientious and decided part, under the evident influence of inflexible integrity and zeal for truth and purity. But his efforts, at that time, had but little success. All our Irish churches had long been in a very low state."[35] Nevertheless, a partial reformation happened at Swift's Alley, as the congregation experienced spiritual renewal. With other help, the congregation also spread the gospel to other parts of Ireland.

The sequel: Robert Fuller
Despite having professed faith while young, Robert Fuller (1782–1809) was a constant source of heartache to his family. He seemed unable to settle to anything, despite a great deal of help from his loving father. Robert became a marine but soon abandoned it. At one point, his father obtained a position for him on a merchant ship, but before sailing, Robert was impressed into the Royal Navy as a sailor on a man-of-war. Shortly afterwards, in June 1801, a report came that he had been found guilty of a misdemeanour and sentenced to three hundred lashes, from which he died. The report turned out to be false, but

---

[34] Morris, *Memoirs*, 104. Swedenborgianism is named after Emanuel Swedenborg (1688–1772), which was theologically Socinian.

[35] Ryland, *Work of Faith*, 230.

one imagines his father's torments while thinking it was true. Three years later, something very similar happened. Ironically, Robert tried to desert in Ireland while his father was there, but he was apprehended and given three hundred and fifty lashes. The punishment was so severe that he became unfit for further service in the navy. On July 6, 1804, Fuller wrote to a friend:

> I arrived at home, last night, well in health; but greatly oppressed with domestic trials. My poor, unhappy son is at Cork. I wrote to him, and he to me, while in Ireland. His letter intimated, that he had but little hopes of living; having a complaint for several months back, in his bowels. He expected to be discharged. I invited him home. Last night, on entering my house, I found all in deep distress; having learnt, by a letter which he wrote to a relation in Cambridgeshire, that his present illness is the effect of having received three hundred and fifty lashes, for desertion. In fact, he is, in a manner, killed! I do not expect his recovery; or, if he should live, that he will ever be able to provide for himself. Yet, if this were but the means of bringing him to God, I should rejoice. Pray for us![36]

Several months later, Robert was discharged and, reaching Bristol, visited his father's old friend John Ryland, Jr. Ryland knew Fuller would be in London the next day and sent Robert to him. Fuller sought to help his son, but Robert went away again, and Fuller lost track of Robert. Fuller eventually discovered that Robert had re-joined the marines. By the end of 1808, Robert wrote a letter of contrition from Brazil to his father. By March 1809, Robert was dead. He died off the coast of Lisbon after a lengthy illness. Later discoveries gave Fuller good reason to believe Robert had come to genuine faith before the end.[37]

---

[36] Ryland, *Work of Faith*, 287. The disease sounds like dysentery, a bacterial infection of the intestines resulting in severe diarrhoea with the presence of blood and mucus in the faeces.

[37] In his final year he attended a Baptist church in Falkirk. When Ryland dealt with the story he expressed the wish that "so affecting an account may be, under a divine blessing, the means of reclaiming some unhappy youth in similar circumstances, or of deterring others" (Ryland, *Work of Faith*, 290).

The excellent Mr. Burls: First London Member of the Committee and Third Treasurer of the Baptist Missionary Society: First Treasurer of the Irish Baptist Society[1]

Ernest A. Payne[2]

When, early in May 1815, Andrew Fuller, the first secretary of the Baptist Missionary Society, lay dying in his manse in Kettering, word was sent to London to the Lothbury counting-house of William Burls—Fuller's "dear friend," as Ryland called him. The Londoner—a man of fifty-two, nine years younger than Fuller—hastened down to Northamptonshire at the end of the week. By then, however, the stricken man was too ill for conversation, and all that William Burls could do was to assure him of his regard and wait with the family for the

---

[1] This article was originally published under the same title in the series of "Brief Biographies of Leading Laymen" by the Carey Press in 1943. While preserving Payne's original text, this reprint has only updated the footnotes. Reprinted with permission.

[2] Ernest Alexander Payne (1902–1980) is a well-known name among Baptist historians. He grew up in Hackney and received his education at Regent's Park College, Mansfield College at the University of Oxford, and the University of Marburg. With his family ties to the Baptist Union, Payne sought to become a Baptist Missionary Society missionary to India. With the mentorship of H. Wheeler Robinson (1872–1945), Payne was ordained at Bugbrooke Baptist Church near Northampton and served as their minister from 1928 to 1932. He then worked for the Baptist Missionary Society as the editorial secretary. From 1940 onwards, Payne served as a senior tutor at Regent's Park College. With his strong support, Regent's Park College moved from London to Oxford and joined the university as a permanent private hall in 1957. Payne also served senior positions in denominational and ecumenical organizations: general secretary of the Baptist Union (1951–1967), moderator of the Free Church Federal Council (1958–1959), and president of the World Council of Churches (1968). Payne published numerous books and journal articles on Baptist history and theology. On Payne's life, see W.M.S. West, *To Be a Pilgrim: A Memoir of Ernest A. Payne* (Guilford, Surrey: Lutterworth, 1983).

end.

Those were sad hours. "You know," wrote Burls, a few days later, "that when he had an important object before him, he steadily pursued it with all his might. It was so with him, even in death. He had to grapple with the King of Terrors: he could think of nothing else."[3] So the Saturday night passed. When the morning came Fuller seemed to revive somewhat, and when he heard singing coming from the chapel next door, he asked to be raised up in bed that he might join, however feebly, in the worship of his people. An hour later, while his young assistant, J.K. Hall, was preaching, Fuller's spirit passed peacefully away. It was William Burls who carried the news from the manse to the chapel. Thence it spread quickly throughout the town and countryside. A prince indeed had fallen in Israel. "The wise, the zealous, the disinterested Secretary of the Baptist Missionary Society—Andrew Fuller—was dead."

In the days that followed heavy responsibilities rested on the shoulders of William Burls. But, as Fuller himself had once said, "Mr. Burls is himself a host." One of his first tasks was to help with the arrangements for the funeral, and he journeyed over to Leicester to break the news to Robert Hall and to ask him to share in the last sad offices. It was Burls who saw to Fuller's personal affairs and who also arranged for the carrying on of the many concerns of the Mission. The secretaryship was placed for the time being in the hands of Dr. Ryland, but he lived in Bristol. The sorting out and transfer of business matters was mainly in Burl's hands. And with this Fuller would have been well content. Fuller knew that some of the friends of the mission had been rather restive under what they deemed his somewhat stern and autocratic manner. He knew it was by no means certain that they would carry out his wishes and make young Christopher Anderson, of Edinburgh, his successor. But he had long known and trusted William Burls, and was confident that such arrangements as he made would be careful and wise and with an eye to the best interests of Carey and the other missionaries.

For some years Burls had acted as a kind of London agent for the mission. He was indeed long the only Londoner on the committee of the society. The B.M.S. was formed in Northamptonshire, and for twenty years its affairs were administered almost exclusively by provincial ministers aided by a small group of laymen whose homes were in Kettering, Birmingham and Nottingham. As the society grew, however, an increasing amount of business had to be transacted in London. Fuller had a countryman's suspicions of the metropolis, but he found in William Burls one in whom he could place complete trust. When he went to London he stayed usually at No. 56, Lothbury, where Burls lived and did his business. The Londoner allowed the missionaries in India to draw their

---

[3] "Obituary. Rev. Andrew Fuller," *Baptist Magazine* 7 (June 1815): 249.

bills upon him, and thus became personally responsible for them. By this and many other acts of generosity, he had shown his zeal for the missionary cause.

At the important annual general meeting of the Society, held in Northampton the autumn after Fuller's death, special thanks were presented to Burls for his "constant, valuable and disinterested services" and he was requested to continue them.[4] The annual meeting the following year was held in Birmingham. It lasted three days and Burls was in the chair throughout the proceedings. He was appointed one of the trustees to hold any surplus funds above £500 and was elected, as representing London, to the sub-committee of nine which was to meet twice a year and act as a kind of executive council. Burls took the chair again in October, 1817, when the full committee of forty-two met in Oxford. Two years later he was called to undertake further special duties. The committee was meeting in Cambridge, and he was appointed co-treasurer with Thomas King, the Birmingham grocer who had, for more than a quarter of a century, been helping to manage the financial affairs of the society. To Burls's action may probably be traced the fact that there soon after appeared the first annual report and statement of accounts in a form somewhat similar to that which we have today. King and Burls resigned in 1821 to make way as treasurer for Benjamin Shaw, M.P., but Burls kept his place on the central committee. His friendship with Fuller, his services to the B.M.S. and his own personality and character alike invite one to seek more information about him.

II

His proves to be an interesting story. Burls is certainly a Baptist layman worthy of remembrance.

He was born in London on March 6th, 1763. This was early in the long reign of George III. It is not easy to picture conditions in a time so distant from our own, but certain contemporary happenings deserve recall. In the early months of 1763 John Wesley was having difficulty with some of his more enthusiastic London followers. To his distress some of them were busy spreading apocalyptic hopes and he records in his diary that, in spite of his protests, on February 28th—less than a week before William Burls was born—"many were afraid to go to bed, and some wandered about in fields, being persuaded that if the world did not end, at least London would be swallowed up by an earthquake."[5] George Whitefield had but recently taken leave of his London friends and was setting out for his sixth visit to America. In May, 1763, when Burls was an infant two months old, Boswell had his first long-desired meeting with the great Dr. Samuel Johnson in a bookseller's shop in Russel Street, Covent Garden.

[4] "Proceedings at Home," *Periodical Accounts, Relative to the Baptist Missionary Society* 5.29 (1814): 683.

[5] John Wesley, *The Journal of John Wesley*, Everyman's Library (London; New York: J.M. Dent, 1913), 3:130.

Sorrow and hardship marked the early years of William Burls. Both his parents died when he was quite young. A place was secured for him, however, at Christ's Hospital—the famous Blue Coat School—then in its old premises near Newgate Street. Our most vivid pictures of this great foundation come from a few years later when Charles Lamb and S.T. Coleridge, and then Leigh Hunt, were there at school. Burls had left before these gifted boys arrived, but he must have been at Christ's Hospital with one who was later to be their close friend, George Dyer, the eccentric minor poet and bookworm, for Dyer's schooldays there lasted from 1762 to 1774.[6] Of Burls's boyish experiences we know no more than that "his attention to his studies and his general good conduct attracted the notice of the master under whose care he was placed and who in various ways manifested his regard."[7]

Early in his teens Burls was apprenticed to a wealthy merchant, John Hankinson, of No. 56 Lothbury. He quickly showed what he could make of this opportunity. His native ability, industry and trustworthiness proved highly advantageous to his master, and John Hankinson readily recognised this and suitably rewarded him. He liked the young man. There came a day when the orphan apprentice was admitted to partnership, and, in 1810, on the death of Hankinson, the business passed altogether into his hands. Burls had become an important figure in the city. This highly successful business career has to be thought of against the background, not only of the Napoleonic wars, but of the industrial revolution as well. Wealth was passing into new hands.

But we must go back somewhat in our story. The earlier years of his association with John Hankinson saw important new developments in Burl's life and interests. He was taken by a friend to Tottenham Court Chapel and passed through a deep and lasting religious experience. Those were the days when what we call the Evangelical Revival was at the peak of its influence, and at Tottenham Court Chapel with its memories of George Whitfield and other evangelical leaders, Burls learnt to conduct himself "soberly, righteously and godly, in this present world," to "love the brotherhood," and to "live, not unto himself, but unto Him that died for him, and rose again." Then, in 1784, at the age of twenty-one, he married one who was to be for more than fifty years his loyal and loving helpmate. For a time they went to Spa Fields Chapel together. Then, because of the situation of their first home, they sat under the ministry of Rowland Hill, the earnest, eloquent, eccentric preacher, for whom Surrey Chapel had been built in 1783. With him they became close friends, but al-

---

[6] See Ernest A. Payne, "The Baptist Connections of George Dyer: Letters to Dr. Rippon from New York," *Baptist Quarterly* 10.5 (1941): 261, and compare E.V. Lucas, *The Life of Charles Lamb*, 3rd ed. (New York; London: G.P. Putman's Sons, 1907), 2:70–83, 239–271.

[7] "Memoir of the Late William Burls, Esq., of Lower Edmonton, Middlesex," *Baptist Magazine* 29 (October 1837): 425.

ready they had begun occasionally to attend the Baptist Chapel in Carter Lane, Southwark. Perhaps it was in the summer months, when Rowland Hill ministered to a congregation in Gloucestershire, that they started to go to Carter Lane. Before many years had passed both Burls and his wife came to Baptist convictions. On March 1st, 1795, they were received as members of the Southwark Church and with it they were closely associated for the next thirty years.

Carter Lane, Southwark, was a strong cause with a notable history stretching back into the seventeenth century. For many years Dr. John Gill, the famous Bible expositor of strict Calvinistic views, had been its minister. He was succeeded in 1773 by John Rippon, well known for his hymn-books and for many other literary and antiquarian ventures, a leading figure in the Baptist life of his day. Connection with the Carter Lane Church must have brought William Burls into touch with many new and stimulating interests. In 1802, when he was in his fortieth year, he was made a deacon.

It is not now possible to discover when William Burls and Andrew Fuller first met. As early as 1798 Burl's name is to be found in the B.M.S. subscription lists, and for nearly forty years his annual guinea was regularly paid. John Hankinson also subscribed from 1798 till his death in 1810, so that in this as in other matters, they saw eye to eye. We know that Fuller was a fairly frequent visitor to the Carter Lane Church. In 1802 the valedictory service for John Chamberlain was held there, and Fuller's address on that occasion was long remembered as specially impressive.[8] By 1805 one of the missionaries in India was writing to William Burls, so that probably by that date he was already doing business for the society. Fuller was frequently in London in 1807, struggling against the difficulties caused by the hostility of the East India Company to the work of the missionaries. Three years later two more B.M.S. recruits had their valedictory service in the Southwark Chapel and at a meeting held there in 1812 the Baptist Union was formed. That was the year of the disastrous Serampore fire, and William Burls, by then sole owner of the business in which he had once been a penniless apprentice, distinguished himself by collecting nearly £1,000 to repair the damage. His subscription list included £15 from himself, £10 from his wife and £5 5s. each from his sons, William and Charles.

In those days Fuller was a frequent visitor at No. 56, Lothbury, and his co-operation with Burls in the affairs of the Mission became increasingly close. As we have seen, Burls had been for some years a member of the B.M.S. Committee. In 1813 came the exhausting agitation over the new East India Charter. In that Burls played no mean part. On March 3rd he went with Fuller, Sutcliff and Ivimey to interview Lord Buckinghamshire, and three weeks later at an im-

---

[8] "Designation of Mr. Chamberlain," *Periodical Accounts Relative to the Baptist Missionary Society* 2.10 (1802): 259, and compare Ernest A. Payne, *The First Generation: Early Leaders of the Baptist Missionary Society in England and India* (London: Carey Press, 1936), 90–96.

portant meeting at the City of London Tavern, with Lord Gambier in the chair, he was added to the widely representative committee which was supporting Wilberforce in his efforts to secure freedom for missionary work in the Company's territories. Those were strenuous months. They may be said to have cost Fuller his life, for even his strong frame began to give way under the strain of all that he sought to do in his Kettering Church, in the service of the B.M.S., and as a theological writer. From then, until his death in 1815, it is clear that Fuller leaned increasingly heavily upon William Burls.

His business and his work for the B.M.S. by no means exhausted William Burls's interests, however. In 1809 he had become one of the committee of the British and Foreign Bible Society. A year or so later he showed himself a keen supporter of the recently formed Baptist Academical Institution at Stepney (out of which grew Regent's Park College); he and his sons were annual subscribers, he was a member of the college committee, and his office was used for the receipt of subscriptions. Then, in 1814, the Baptist Irish Society was founded. It aimed at spreading the Gospel in Ireland and grew out of an initial evangelistic journey undertaken under B.M.S. auspices. Of the new Society William Burls was made treasurer and Joseph Ivimey secretary. Ivimey was minister of the well-known Baptist Church meeting in Eagle Street, Holborn. Here indeed were enterprises enough for one man.

The work of the Baptist Irish Society, in which Burls took a very deep interest, deserves, perhaps, an additional word or so, for it long ago ceased its operations and its story is little known. In the early years of the nineteenth century evangelical Christians felt considerable concern about the state of affairs in Ireland. The London Hibernian Society promoted schools, and the Irish Evangelical Society employed itinerant preachers, both bodies being on an interdenominational basis. In 1814 the Baptist Society for Promoting the Gospel in Ireland was formed at the New London Tavern. The B.M.S. made an initial gift of £21 to its funds, and Fuller a personal one of five guineas. Joseph Ivimey and Christopher Anderson undertook an extensive journey through Ireland and, before long, the new society had three or four itinerant preachers employed and was organising schools on "the circulating, or ambulatory plan" and busily engaged in distributing Scripture portions. In the schools the Irish language was extensively taught. Inevitably there came opposition from the Roman Catholic priests and charges of proselytism. Poverty as well as ignorance reigned in Ireland in the first half of the nineteenth century and to them, before long, was added violence. The agents of the Baptist Irish Society had a very difficult time. Their work, however, created a good deal of interest in Baptist circles. The breakfast of the Society was the concluding gathering of the Baptist annual meetings, held then in June. It took place usually at the London Tavern. The supporters of the Society had to be there at six o'clock in the morning. The proceedings began at seven a.m. and the doors were then opened to the general public, who came in to hear the speeches. It is recorded that in 1817 "upwards of 500 took breakfast and about 1,000 attended," over £300 being raised for the funds of the Society.[9] At these annual gatherings the chair was usually taken by Joseph Butterworth, M.P. for Coventry. If he could not come, then invariably William Burls, the treasurer, was called upon. The reports of the meetings make clear the respect and affection in which he was held, and show that he was an admirable chairman, a man of few words and those direct and businesslike.

III

The decade from 1814 to 1824 was undoubtedly the busiest and most influential in the life of this devoted Baptist layman. Lothbury and Carter Lane, Kettering and Stepney, India and Ireland—all claimed his constant attention. Suddenly all this activity had to cease. On October 14th, 1824, as he was rising from family prayers, he had a severe stroke. Ours is not the first generation in which the zealous and conscientious may attempt too much.

Burls was then only in his sixty-second year. His left side was paralysed, and for some time his life hung in the balance. So dismayed were his friends at the prospect of his death that special prayer meetings for his recovery were held at Carter Lane and Eagle Street. He was nursed devotedly by his wife, and slowly, though he never regained his physical powers, his mind cleared. The eleventh annual meeting of the Baptist Irish Society, held in June, 1825, gave special thanks "for the restoration, though partial," of its treasurer, after his "long and alarming illness."[10] His son, William, had been helping with the affairs of the Society and was that same year appointed one of the auditors of the B.M.S. But Burls's own active career was at an end. He could no longer carry on his business, and he had to resign from the many committees on which he had served. It was significant of the gratitude and regard in which he was held in B.M.S. circles that for a further eight years his name was retained on the B.M.S. committee, though he could take no active part in its deliberations.

This was a testing experience. Yet Burls was soon writing to a friend: "Amidst this affliction many and great mercies have been granted, so that the mercies preponderated."[11]

He moved from Lothbury out to Edmonton, and had his membership transferred to the recently formed Baptist Church at High Road, Tottenham, not

---

[9] "Baptist Irish Society," *Baptist Magazine* 9 (July 1817): 279.

[10] "Speeches at the Eleventh Anniversary of the Baptist Irish Society," *Baptist Magazine* 17 (August 1825): 358.

[11] "Memoir of the Late William Burls," 429.

clinging on for sentimental reasons to associations at Carter Lane. He could not often join in public worship, but he continued deeply and generously interested in the causes to which he had given so much time and energy. As he looked back over his life he was full of gratitude to God for His guidance and grace. In spite of sad weakness of body he did not repine or complain. The depth and genuineness of his religion were clearly shown. His friends at Carter Lane had always known him as a man of prayer and he had regarded himself as no more than steward of his possessions and talents.

For no less than thirteen years he lived thus, a stricken but not a defeated man. The curtain was gradually descending on the labours of a generation—one of the outstanding generations in English history. In 1833 Charles and Mary Lamb came to be his neighbours in Edmonton, and there in December, 1834, the gentle, whimsical Charles passed away. Perhaps in those last months both he and William Burls turned back in memory to their schooldays at Christ's Hospital. That same year William Carey and Joseph Ivimey died. Two years later, Burls's old pastor, John Rippon, passed away. In the spring of 1837, the youngest daughter died very suddenly in the home at Edmonton. Slowly Burls's own strength departed. The end came on June 26th, 1837. "He descended the dark valley by easy and gentle steps, and crossed the flood in peace." Less than a week earlier King William IV had died, leaving his youthful niece, Victoria, to ascend the throne of England, and before the year was out, Joshua Marshman, the last of the great Serampore trio, had gone to his reward. A new age was beginning.

Both Ivimey and Rippon had been buried in Bunhill Fields, Finsbury, that spot where rest the mortal remains of so many of the heroic figures of English Nonconformity from Bunyan and Fox onwards. There the body of William Burls was carried. His active service must have seemed a rather distant memory, but all knew that he had been the trusted friend and colleague of Fuller and Ryland and many other giants of the past. The secretary of the B.M.S., John Dyer, spoke at the graveside, taking as his text "Be followers of them who through faith and patience inherit the promises." Faith and patience, both words were apt in the case of William Burls. The B.M.S. *Annual Report*, presented in the spring of 1838, in noting his decease used an expressive phrase which says much for the position he had secured and maintained in the hearts of his friends—"the excellent Mr. Burls."[12]

There is no accessible portrait of William Burls. The records about him have been so long covered with dust that even his name is unfamiliar save to a few. He was not one of the major figures of his day. Nevertheless, he deserves a

---

[12] *The Annual Report of the Committee of the Baptist Missionary Society, Addressed to the General Meeting, Held at Finsbury Chapel, Thursday, Mat 3rd, 1838. Being a Continuation of the Periodical Accounts Relative to the Society* (London: Baptist Missionary Society General Meeting, 1838), 34.

place in this series of brief biographies, for he was certainly one of the leading Baptist laymen of the time, and he may be taken as the representative of a notable group. His contemporaries, William Fox, the draper of Gloucestershire and London, and William Brodie Gurney, the shorthand-writer and philanthropist, both find a place in the Dictionary of National Biography. Joseph Gutteridge was well known far beyond London Baptist circles. In the provinces the B.M.S. received yeoman service from men like Thomas Potts and Thomas King, of Birmingham, James Lomax, of Nottingham, and William Hope, of Liverpool. All are worthy of recall, yet none is perhaps able to speak to the present generation so clearly and effectively as William Burls.

Hannah Marshman: A founding missionary of the Serampore Mission

Sydney Dixon

Sydney Dixon is a pseudonym for a missionary currently serving in a closed country.

Hannah Marshman (1767–1847) gave her life as an integral member of the seminal Baptist Missionary Society's mission at Serampore. Along with her husband, Joshua Marshman (1768–1837), Hannah served as an unofficial founding missionary alongside William Carey (1761–1834) and William Ward (1769–1823). The individual tasks of the first missionaries varied. However, each individual's contribution necessarily propelled the Serampore Mission toward significantly influencing mission history across the sub-continent and beyond. This article will supply a foundational biographical account of Hannah Marshman's life by tracing her life and circumstances from Great Britain's missionary awakening through her life in Serampore, Bengal, India, where she devoted forty-seven years of service in the Christian missionary enterprise.

Hannah's context—British Baptists of the eighteenth century
With the Act of Toleration (1689), eighteenth-century English Baptists experienced new levels of freedom in public worship and societal engagements. However, political toleration remained limited as all varieties of dissenters experienced continued political oppression.[1] Despite the ongoing political difficulties faced by English Baptists, they placed immense value on living life as an

---

[1] Raymond Brown, *The English Baptists of the Eighteenth Century* (London: Baptist Historical Society, 1986), 3; J.H.Y. Briggs, "Baptists and the Wider Community" in *Challenge and Change: English Baptist Life in the Eighteenth Century*, ed. Stephen Copson and Peter J. Morden (Didcot, Oxfordshire: Baptist Historical Society, 2017), 123–129.

expression of their faith.

Theological practice permeated every facet of Baptist life, including their interactions with other Christians. David Thompson writes, "since all Baptists affirmed that 'church power' lay within the local congregation and nowhere else, relations with other Christians began with the local church."[2] The evangelical movement of the 1730s affected British dissenters in varying ways. Even though Thompson asserts that the formation and influence of the Baptist Missionary Society (BMS) in 1792 mark evangelicalism's appearance in "formal Baptist organisations," Baptist life preceding Hannah's birth gives evidence to evangelical influence.[3]

For these Baptists, they saw everything as "an expression of their spirituality: not only *what* they believed but *who* they believed and *how* they sought to bear witness to the grace of God."[4] Thus, English Baptists' Christian faith permeated every corner of their existent. The family stood at the centre of the practice and demonstration of the Baptist faith. Karen Smith traces Baptist familial structures from their Puritan fathers stating, "They believed that family life had been ordained by God, and the home was the place where the structure and moral fibre of society was taught and monitored … The insistence on following what they believed to be the divine order in relationships shaped" their lives.[5] The frailty of life in the eighteenth century meant dealing with frequent deaths within the family. Smith writes, "The accepted theological and spiritual response was simply that the loss of children to disease and sickness was 'God's will' or indeed a means of testing or punishing parents, which thus had to be faced and accepted."[6] To the Baptist mind, as to many dissenters, the structure and discipline of the family lie staunchly under the sovereignty of God.

Literacy and education maintained a vital place within eighteenth-century Baptist life. Faith and Brian Bowers write that because "dissenting churches valued literacy, wanting people to read the Bible," ministers often opened and led schools as a form of secular occupation.[7] However, Baptists increasingly looked

---

[2] David Thompson, "Baptists in the Eighteenth Century: Relations with Other Christians" in *Challenge and Change*, 263.

[3] Brown, *English Baptists of the Eighteenth Century*, 76–77; Thompson, "Baptists in the Eighteenth Century," 279.

[4] Christopher J. Ellis, "The Beauty of Social Religion: Local Baptist Life in the Eighteenth Century" in *Challenge and Change*, 78.

[5] Karen E. Smith, "Baptists at Home" in *Challenge and Change*, 101, 103.

[6] Smith, "Baptists at Home," 122.

[7] Faith Bowers and Brian Bowers, "After the Benediction: Eighteenth-Century Baptist Laity" in *Challenge and Change*, 234.

to education as an essential part of faith practice. Timothy Whelan states that "most eighteenth-century Baptists viewed education and the study of literature and the arts (especially poetry) as legitimate vehicles by which they could demonstrate and articulate their faith."[8] Education and spirituality comingled within Baptist life. The importance of education bore itself out in the establishment of educational institutions within the denomination. The Bristol Baptist Academy (est. 1720) cultivated "moderate Calvinism, a love for the Scriptures, and a commitment to a missional piety."[9] The Baptists created various avenues of theological training during this century. However, the Bristol Baptist Academy looms large among them. Michael A.G. Haykin notes the broad view of education adopted, noting that "there was also a great emphasis at Bristol on the cultivation of Christian spirituality and practice in preaching and itinerant evangelism."[10] Institutions for theological education existed outside Bristol (such as Olney and Stepney). However, Haykin notes, "The impact of the Bristol Academy on the growth and revitalization of the Particular Baptists in the final decades of the long eighteenth century cannot be overstated."[11] Association through pastoral training schools was not the only effective association among Particular Baptists. A "moderate form of Calvinism, with its vigorous evangelistic activity, began to be disseminated among the Particular Baptists at this time through the renewed life of the Associations."[12] It acknowledged that sound doctrine must be coupled with evangelistic action.[13]

An emphasis on education was not limited to pastoral training. Baptists developed catechisms and Sunday Schools for their children.[14] Sunday Schools helped to increase literacy but were mainly meant to "spread the religion of Jesus."[15] A shift in the situation for females is most evident through the door of education among girls and in the number of women running schools.[16] Smith

---

[8] Timothy Whelan, "'No Sanctuary for Philistines': Baptists and Culture in the Eighteenth Century" in *Challenge and Change*, 207.

[9] Brown, *English Baptists of the Eighteenth Century*, 72; Peter J. Morden, "Continuity and Change: Particular Baptists in the 'Long Eighteenth Century' (1689–1815)" in *Challenge and Change*, 3.

[10] Michael A.G. Haykin, "'With Light, Beauty, and Power': Educating English Baptists in the Long Eighteenth Century" in *Challenge and Change*, 186; Brown, *English Baptists of the Eighteenth Century*, 84.

[11] Haykin, "'With Light, Beauty, and Power,'" 187.

[12] Brown, *English Baptists of the Eighteenth Century*, 85.

[13] Brown, *English Baptists of the Eighteenth Century*, 86.

[14] Brown, *English Baptists of the Eighteenth Century*, 48, 51–52.

[15] Haykin, "'With Light, Beauty, and Power,'" 201.

[16] Smith, "Baptists at Home," 121.

notes, "By the end of the century, with the formation of the Particular Baptist Society for the Propagation of the Gospel Amongst the Heathen (1792), women would begin to take a more active role in mission work and education in the churches."[17] Education played a formative role in the gospel's spread and the participation of every member (including women) in gospel work.

Hannah Shepherd was born in southwest England into a Baptist family living through the denominational changes of the eighteenth century. Steeped in the Baptist tradition, Hannah's life demonstrates the effects of shifts among the Baptists and their evolving religious expression. Together with the perspective that eighteenth-century English Baptist life built into young Hannah, events in her personal life shaped her into a resilient woman whose legacy looms large within the Serampore Mission story.

Hannah's life before Serampore (1767–1799)

Before Hannah's arrival in India, her life passed through three distinct phases. Hannah was born into a nuclear family clinging to its Baptist root until great tragedy struck. When grave misfortunes ripped apart her family, Hannah unexpectedly met with circumstances proving to be blessings of the Divine. Finally, near the end of the century, Hannah married her life's partner—in martial union and service to God—and they sailed to India together.

Hannah was born on May 13, 1767, in Bristol as the only daughter of John (a farmer) and Rachel Shepherd. She received intermittent education due to her family's frequent moves and her mother's illness. During Rachel Shepherd's battle with consumption, the family endured the tragic death of their youngest son in 1772.[18] The Shepherds continued life with their two remaining children until 1779. Two years her senior, Hannah's brother Godfrey entertained his little sister on Saturdays, events which Hannah recalled to the day of her death.[19] During the French Revolution (1789–1799), Godfrey experienced a harrowing escape on the continent and, later, a life cut short in Jamacia.[20] Godfrey's dramatic life was not the first instance of great calamity in Hannah's life, and Godfrey's removal to distant countries was not the first separation of the siblings.

Rachel Shepherd's consumption appeared around the time of her youngest son's death in 1772. As her mother's disease progressed, Hannah remained

---

[17] Smith, "Baptists at Home," 122.

[18] Rachel Voigt, "Memoir of Mrs. Hannah Marshman's Earlier Years," Box IN/20, BMS Archives (Angus Library and Archives, Regent's Park College, Oxford), 4. The unpublished manuscript was compiled by Hannah Marshman's daughter, Rachel Voigt.

[19] Voigt, "Memoir of Mrs. Hannah Marshman's Earlier Years," 3.

[20] Voigt, "Memoir of Mrs. Hannah Marshman's Earlier Years," 3–4.

by her side as a "constant companion and nurse."[21] After a three-year battle, Hannah's mother died in 1775. Until the end of her own life, Hannah recalled, "the mildness, gentleness, and resignation which marked her mother's last sufferings."[22] Because she was close to her mother, especially during the years she played nursemaid, her loss marked the beginning of increased difficulty for young Hannah. Unable to recover from his wife's death, John Shepherd sent his children to live with others. The move to her paternal uncle's home marked a period of constant transiency among the homes of various family and friends.[23] In 1779, in debt, Hannah's father also succumbed to illness in death. Upon her own deathbed, Hannah recounted her father's struggle, "the removal of my dear mother so sensibly affected my father's health, that he never fully recovered the stroke."[24] At the age of twelve, Hannah became an orphan.

Hannah spent the remainder of her childhood shuffling between extended family and friends. Throughout her childhood, education came through both formal and informal avenues. Hannah's time with her grandfather, John Clark (1711–1803), afforded her the "benefit of his instructions in secular knowledge, and his wisdom and experience in spiritual attainments."[25] Despite all the difficulties Hannah experienced during her childhood, she recalled the years with her grandfather as some of the happiest in her life.[26]

Hannah's grandfather, John Clark

John Clark pastored the Baptist congregation at Crockerton in Wiltshire for nearly sixty years.[27] Although Clark's parents belonged to a Baptist congregation in Frome, Somersetshire, at the time of his birth on December 29, 1711, it was only at the age of nineteen that Clark submitted himself to God.[28] Two years before his death, Clark penned the words of his testimony, writing:

---

[21] Voigt, "Memoir of Mrs. Hannah Marshman's Earlier Years," 4.

[22] Voigt, "Memoir of Mrs. Hannah Marshman's Earlier Years," 4.

[23] Voigt, "Memoir of Mrs. Hannah Marshman's Earlier Years," 4.

[24] W.H. Denham, "Memoir of the Late Mrs. Marshman, Widow of the Late Dr. Joshua Marshman of Serampore: From the Funeral Address Delivered March 14, 1847, by the Rev. W. H. Denham," *Baptist Magazine* 10 (August 1847): 478.

[25] Voigt, "Memoir of Mrs. Hannah Marshman's Earlier Years," 4.

[26] Voigt, "Memoir of Mrs. Hannah Marshman's Earlier Years," 3–4.

[27] John Clark Marshman, *The Life and Times of Carey, Marshman, and Ward: Embracing the History of the Serampore Mission* (London: Longman, Brown, Green, Longmans, & Roberts, 1859), 1:106; Anonymous, "Memoir of the Exemplary Life and Comfortable Death of The Late Rev. John Clark, Pastor of the Baptist Church at Crockerton, Wilts.," *Evangelical Magazine* 11 (November 1803): 464.

[28] "Memoir of Rev. John Clark," 461.

> I was convinced of my sinful ruined state, and was filled with distress, bordering on despair … I thought the clouds appeared charged with the wrath of God; and feared they would burst on my head and sink me into endless ruin. In this awful state I continued about eighteen days; but one day, being alone, lamenting my miserable helpless condition, these words occurred to my mind, "My grace is sufficient for thee." The impression was so forcible, that I verily thought some one behind me had spoken them, and turned round to see who it was; but no one was there … but soon recollected that it was a part of Scripture; and began to think, Who can tell but what there may be hope for me? … While meditating on these things, there appeared to my mind such fulness and sufficiency in Christ, and in what he had done to save sinners, that I thought I could rest my soul on him for life and salvation; and from that time I found my mind relieved from the dreadful burden that had oppressed it.[29]

After a time of fellowship with the Baptist congregation in Frome, Clark moved to Bath, where no Baptist congregation yet existed. In Bath, Clark and a few like-minded Christians gathered for informal worship. In the bosom of this intimate group, Clark's pastoral skills developed, and when the Crockerton congregation fell in need of a pastor, they called Clark to fill the role.[30] The 1803 memoir of Clark, published in *The Evangelical Magazine*, records Hannah, the daughter of Clark's eldest child (of four), as one of his eleven grandchildren and the "wife of one of the Missionaries at Serampore."[31] John Clark lived to the age of 93, and died on April 5, 1803.

The news of John Shepherd's death prompted Clark to arrange for her to live with her aunt, Hannah Clark. Eventually, the two Hannahs resided with the reverend.[32] After three years, fifteen-year-old Hannah attended family friends to Devonshire Square in London.[33] Unfortunately, Hannah began to suffer significantly from the very illness that took her mother's life. After two years of struggling with consumption, Hannah returned to her grandfather's home.[34] Hannah's daughter, Rachel Voigt, describes Hannah's devotion to God during the years of her illness, writing, "Prayer, secret and social, meditation

---

[29] "Memoir of Rev. John Clark," 461–462.

[30] "Memoir of Rev. John Clark," 462.

[31] "Memoir of Rev. John Clark," 463.

[32] Voigt, "Memoir of Mrs. Hannah Marshman's Earlier Years," 4.

[33] Voigt, "Memoir of Mrs. Hannah Marshman's Earlier Years," 5.

[34] Voigt, "Memoir of Mrs. Hannah Marshman's Earlier Years," 5.

and attendance on God's ordinances became her meat and drink."[35] The reputation of a life devoted to prayer characterized Hannah until the end of her earthly life.

Hannah became convicted of her need for a Saviour during her grave illness. Upon her recovery, Hannah happily received baptism administered by Robert Marshman (1763–1806) at Westbury Leigh in Wiltshire.[36] During the seven years that followed, Hannah passed between her grandfather's home and the home of family friends who had lost their only child and requested Hannah's company.[37] Hannah became acquainted with Joshua Marshman through family friends.[38]

Joshua Marshman

John and Mary (née Couzener) Marshman welcomed their son, Joshua, on April 20, 1768, in Westbury Leigh. The Marshmans were members of the Baptist congregation at Westbury Leigh, and in Joshua's seventh year his father entertained him with the story of David, sparking a great interest in the stories of the Bible.[39] Joshua became a mostly self-taught reader and student of Old Testament narratives. He developed into an avid reader who would travel far and wide to borrow books and read more than five hundred before his eighteenth birthday.[40]

When living in his father's home, Joshua worked as a weaver. At fifteen, he moved to Holborn in London to work for a Mr. Cator, a bookseller.[41] However, after only five months, Joshua's father recalled him home, where he continued to work as a weaver. Through a personal study of the Scriptures, Joshua gradually experienced "the light of divine truth ... and he was enabled to place his entire dependence for acceptance with God, and his hope of eternal salvation,

---

[35] Voigt, "Memoir of Mrs. Hannah Marshman's Earlier Years," 5.

[36] Voigt, "Memoir of Mrs. Hannah Marshman's Earlier Years," 6; Sunil Kumar Chatterjee, *Hannah Marshman: The First Woman Missionary in India* (Hooghly, India: Sri Sunil Chatterjee, 2006), 28; Denham, "Memoir of Mrs. Marshman," 479. The accounts of familial relation between Robert Marshman and Joshua Marshman are inconsistent. However, the majority opinion is that they were not related.

[37] Voigt, "Memoir of Mrs. Hannah Marshman's Earlier Years," 6.

[38] Voigt, "Memoir of Mrs. Hannah Marshman's Earlier Years," 6; Denham, "Memoir of Mrs. Marshman," 478.

[39] Edward Ashton, "A Lecture on Joshua Marshman" (Westbury Leigh: Westbury Leigh Baptist Church, 1929); Marshman, *Life and Times*, 1:99–100.

[40] Ashton, "Lecture on Joshua Marshman"; Marshman, *Life and Times*, 1:100; Voigt, "Memoir of Mrs. Hannah Marshman's Earlier Years," 15.

[41] Ashton, "Lecture on Joshua Marshman"; Marshman, *Life and Times*, 1:102–104.

on the all meritorious atonement of Christ."[42] After a deeper study of Martin Luther's (1483–1546) commentaries and Puritan devotions, "he was still unable to come up to the high standard of the church at Westbury Leigh"—a fact lamented by Edward Ashton, pastor of Westbury Leigh, in 1929.[43] The leadership of the Baptist congregation at Westbury Leigh looked with suspicion upon the educational pursuits of ministers, considering it a dangerous path to developing "men-made ministers."[44] Thus, they held Joshua in an observatory state for seven years, never giving him baptism and full acceptance into the congregation.[45]

In 1794—during the third year of his marriage to Hannah—with permission from the Westbury Leigh deacons, Joshua took a position in Bristol at the school supported by the Broadmead congregation.[46] Upon mutual acquaintance, John Ryland (1793–1825) urged Joshua's baptism into Broadmead. For five years, Joshua taught at the school and attended the Bristol Academy, becoming one of the many students who "brought an outstanding contribution to the life of the churches in the second half of the eighteenth century."[47] When Carey's call for more missionaries to join him in India came, Joshua's friend, William Grant (d. 1807), offered to answer the call. Joshua added his name alongside Grant's, and three weeks later, the Marshmans began their journey to India. When Joshua's feet touched the shores of Bengal, he fell to his knees to give thank to God for the party's safe arrival.[48]

Hannah and Joshua's relationship: The early years
Hannah and Joshua met through mutual friends and married at Bratton Church on August 8, 1791.[49] Their 46-year marriage persisted until Joshua's death in 1837. Together, they had six children who lived into adulthood. Before their marriage, during her seven-year-round-robin residency, moving between her grandfather's home and family friends, Hannah lived in Westbury Leigh. Some claim that Hannah lived in the older part of a house that also contained a

---

[42] Marshman, *Life and Times*, 1:104–105.

[43] Ashton, "Lecture on Joshua Marshman"; Marshman, *Life and Times*, 1:105; Voigt, "Memoir of Mrs. Hannah Marshman's Earlier Years," 15.

[44] Marshman, *Life and Times*, 1:105–106.

[45] Ashton, "Lecture on Joshua Marshman"; Marshman, *Life and Times*, 1:104–105.

[46] Ashton, "Lecture on Joshua Marshman"; Marshman, *Life and Times*, 1:107.

[47] Brown, *English Baptists of the Eighteenth Century*, 84.

[48] Marshman, *Life and Times*, 1:111; Voigt, "Memoir of Mrs. Hannah Marshman's Earlier Years," 23.

[49] Voigt, "Memoir of Mrs. Hannah Marshman's Earlier Years," 6.

school where she worked as a teacher.[50] After their marriage, the young couple remained in Westbury Leigh until moving to Bristol for Joshua's position at the Broadmead school. During their years in Bristol, Ryland advised Joshua to become a student at the Bristol Academy, and they later became missionaries to India.

When Carey's request came for more missionary families to join him in Bengal, while Joshua was studying at Bristol, Hannah expressed serious objections to leaving Bristol. One story persists that Hannah denied Joshua's suit for marriage until he promised she would not have to leave England.[51] At first, Hannah expressed doubt "as to whether it was the path of duty, to break up every association and leave so useful and happy a sphere at home."[52] Joshua later recalled this affair for his children, writing:

> Dr. Ryland had long wished my mind might be stirred up to go [to India], although he had felt delicate in hinting this to me. He now advised me to make it a matter of earnest prayer, and thought I might rely on this as a token of God's approbation, namely if your dear mother engaged therein with all her heart. To my astonishment and joy, she on weighing things entered most cordially into the missionary undertaking, and although we were in so pleasing a situation as to worldly things, ... your dear Mother, from love to the Redeemer, gave up all for the sake of His cause in India. Oh may He bless her to her latest hour, and grant her and me, unworthy as I am, to inherit together everlasting life through his own infinite merits.[53]

Sunil Chatterjee surmises the influence of Ryland upon Hannah's consent to offer their family into the Lord's service in India: "Probably Dr. Ryland's inspiring encouragement helped her to take the final decision of joining her husband in missionary undertaking. Moreover she had within herself not only [a] genuine religious spirit but also an urge to dedicate to serve for the cause of God, denying her own comfort and happiness."[54] Ultimately, Hannah became the longest serving member of the original Baptist missionaries at Serampore.

The Marshmans left their homeland within three weeks of their application. Their family had already suffered the terrible loss of two children. First,

---

[50] Ashton, "Lecture on Joshua Marshman"; Chatterjee, *Hannah Marshman*, 28.

[51] Voigt, "Memoir of Mrs. Hannah Marshman's Earlier Years," 7.

[52] Voigt, "Memoir of Mrs. Hannah Marshman's Earlier Years," 7.

[53] Voigt, "Memoir of Mrs. Hannah Marshman's Earlier Years," 8; Marshman, *Life and Times*, 1:107.

[54] Chatterjee, *Hannah Marshman*, 32.

their three-year-old daughter, Mary (d. 1795); then two years later, an infant son died.[55] Life in India would not spare them recurring visits of death upon their family. However, in 1799, the Marshmans' two living children accompanied them to India, who were John Clark Marshman (1794–1877) and Susan (1798–1822).[56]

The voyage to India and arrival at Serampore (1799)
On May 29, 1799, the new missionary party embarked for India. The Marshmans were joined by William Ward, Charles Grant and his wife, Daniel Brunsdon and his wife, Mary Tidd, who travelled with them as the finance of John Fountain, already working with Carey in Bengal, and the eight children of their collective families. Joshua's journals record that during the long and difficult voyage, many in their number endured prolonged and grave sickness.

From the start of their missionary service, the Marshmans demonstrated an attitude of marital partnership in ministry that mirrored an important missionary requirement laid out by Carey. In his request to the BMS for more workers, Carey writes: "it is absolutely necessary for the wives of the missionaries to be as hearty in the work of their husbands."[57] A journal entry, dated September 1, 1799, opens a small window into the Marshmans' understanding of marital partnership in family structure and ministry. Joshua wrote: "had a long conversation with H[annah] about the nature of our calling, and our duty towards each other and above all loving those who are connected with us in the Lord's bonds."[58] Hannah put hands and feet to their duty to care for those connected to them even while aboard the *Criterion* and struggling with her own illness. From the beginning of October, as their voyage was coming to an end, Grant's wife became deadly ill. Joshua's journals recount their grave concern for Mrs. Grant and his great admiration for Hannah in her care for Mrs. Grant.[59] These trying events demonstrate a perspective of shared ministry infused with Joshua's sweet affection for his wife. They also provide a foreshadowing of the life to come at Serampore.

Immediate relief from their difficult circumstances did not coincide with their arrival upon the shores of Bengal. The new missionaries expected to face some level of harassment at the hands of the British government and officials of the East India Company due to the general hostility they held toward

---

[55] Voigt, "Memoir of Mrs. Hannah Marshman's Earlier Years," 7.

[56] Voigt, "Memoir of Mrs. Hannah Marshman's Earlier Years," 7.

[57] Marshman, *Life and Times*, 1:78.

[58] Voigt, "Memoir of Mrs. Hannah Marshman's Earlier Years," 21.

[59] Voigt, "Memoir of Mrs. Hannah Marshman's Earlier Years," 22–23.

missionaries and their unlicensed intent of missionary action in India.[60] As a pre-emptive measure, the new missionaries approached Calcutta with letters proving an invitation and indicating their intent to disembark at Serampore, a Danish settlement thirty kilometres north of Calcutta.[61] Although the political drama of their arrival at Serampore on October 13, 1799, did not immediately resolve, in the end, the missionaries were allowed to settle at Serampore under Danish protection. Their hardships were not contained in the political sphere. Personal tragedy landed ashore with them. A mere eighteen days after their arrival, on October 31, 1799, Grant died, leaving behind a widow and two young daughters.[62] Within a short time, the Carey family joined them in Serampore, bringing their own trauma-induced drama.[63] Chatterjee credits Carey's later observation of Hannah's endurance of the many odd and difficult situations to his earlier request to the BMS to send wives equally ready to work alongside their husbands.[64] After the death and birth within their newly landed party, the arrival of the Carey family put their group at ten adults and nine children.

Hannah's life at Serampore (1799–1847)
During their years in Serampore, the Marshmans increased to a family of eight and eventually added children-in-law and grandchildren. However, with their settlement at Serampore, the families operated as one large, collective mission family. They shared the intimacies of joint-family living, sharing a common dwelling space, and collective family operations in domestic and ministry life. The mission work followed a set of shared objectives yet fell into a natural division of labor among the Serampore missionaries. As the "mother of the mission," Hannah acquired immense domestic responsibilities for the missionary

---

[60] Kenneth Ballhatchet, "The East India Company and Roman Catholic Missionaries," *Journal of Ecclesiastical History* 44.2 (1993): 288. Christian missionary activity on the Indian subcontinent began with the arrival of St. Thomas in the first century. Subsequent Christian activity in India remained mainly in the South, with small ingresses by Catholic missionaries whom the East India Company welcomed to serve pre-existing Indian Catholics and Irish soldiers. As the East Indian Company and British authorities established and continued to expand their authority in India, missionary activity was banned without a dedicated license from the government, which the authorities were extremely hesitant to grant to Protestants. Thus, until 1813 when Protestant missionaries were officially allowed entry, Christian missionaries operated illegally in British India.

[61] Marshman, *Life and Times*, 1:110–11.

[62] Voigt, "Memoir of Mrs. Hannah Marshman's Earlier Years," 29. The two orphan daughters of Mr. Grant—Kitty and Phoebe—were brought up by Hannah after the death of their mother in 1806.

[63] Marshman, *Life and Times*, 1:301. William Carey arrived at Serampore with four young sons and an insane wife in tow. Dorothy Carey's crippled mental state persisted for twelve years, until her death in 1807. With a completely mentally absent mother, Hannah took on the mothering necessities for the Carey sons.

[64] Chatterjee, *Hannah Marshman*, 40.

household, which gained even greater levels with the shifting circumstances of life in India. Hannah's ministerial roles extended to some degree outside the mission premises to the native and European communities and even back in England. In 1825, a report from Serampore lamented that even though Hannah was in her twilight years, the mission required her intense labours to manage its functionality.[65] In all, Hannah gave birth to twelve children, yet tragically only six lived past infancy, and five survived their mother. Aside from John Clark and Susan—the two living children who travelled from England—two more daughters and two sons completed the Marshman family in Serampore.[66]

In a 1797 letter to the BMS seeking to recruit additional missionary labour for India, Carey proposed the establishment of a settlement modelled after the Moravians, as Carey explained: "we ought to be seven or eight families together … all living together … having nothing of our own, but all the general stock."[67] He further proposed that the group elect stewards from among them to

---

[65] A. Christopher Smith, "The Legacy of William Ward and Joshua and Hannah Marshman," *International Bulletin of Missionary Research* 23.3 (1999): 128.

[66] In John Clark Marshman's biography, he summarises his siblings' stations in life, offering few details about his two younger brothers. He describes the second brother as a failed solicitor and the youngest as following a life path in England (Marshman, *Life and Times*, 2:520). Chatterjee notes the *Friend of India* weekly series dated March 1847 as a source naming Benjamin as the second Marshman son who became an attorney and member of Tumner and Marshman in Calcutta but later settling in Agra (Chatterjee, *Hannah Marshman*, 71, 76). Rachel, the Marshmans' second living daughter, married a Danish doctor, Joachim Otto Voigt (1795–1843), who served as the medical officer at Serampore, and later the superintendent of forests in British Burma (Marshman, *Life and Times*, 2:517). The Marshman's youngest daughter, Hannah, married Major-General Sir Henry Havelock (1795–1857). Havelock later became a Baptist and was baptised by John Mack at Serampore. During her husband's military service, Hannah and her two sons narrowly escaped death in a house fire.

Biographical accounts of the Marshmans hold the most information on the two eldest children. John Clark Marshman (1794–1877) arrived in Serampore as a young child but quickly grew into a dedicated assistant and co-laborer in the mission. By the end of his life, John Clark found recognition as a talented journalist and historian. During his years with the Mission, he helped to establish the first newspaper in the Bengali language and the *Friend of India* periodical. His major historical works include a two-volume tome, *The Life and Times of Carey, Marshman, and Ward*, and a history of British India, *The History of India*. He returned to England in 1852, where he continued to write (Anonymous, "The Late Mr. J. C. Marshman," *Illustrated London News* 71 [July 28, 1877]: 98). He died in 1877 at the age of eighty-two.

Susan Marshman Williams (1798–1822) was born in England but spent most of her years in India. Susan married Henry Allan Williams (1788–1823), employed in the Bengal civil service and a commercial resident of Jungypore. After little more than three years of marriage and two children, Susan died of fever. Later, Susan's daughter died of consumption at the age of twenty, and the Williams's son suffered mental health issues related to his military service with the East India Company (Marshman, *Life and Times*, 2:250). Marshman describes his sister as "a woman of unaffected piety … and peculiar sweetness" (Marshman, *Life and Times*, 2:250–251). When Susan died, Joshua Marshman mourned deeply and continued to write daily to his son-in-law for two years, up until Williams' death (Marshman, *Life and Times*, 2:251).

[67] Marshman, *Life and Times*, 1:78–79.

manage set rules regarding "eating, drinking, worship, working, learning, preaching excursions."[68] Although the location and various details bore out differently than Carey's original vision, the Moravian lifestyle he proposed became much of the reality the original Serampore missionary families lived. Within the arrangements for their shared life, the missionary wives received charge of keeping the household accounts. Hannah—the most senior, and mentally healthy woman among them—became the mother of the mission, taking charge of the entire mission household. Hannah's letters describe the mission family's daily life regarding food and family customs, demonstrating the frugality of their collective lifestyle so that they could perpetuate the mission by all means possible.[69] Noting how the individual families' incomes were substantially higher than the amount they retained, Chatterjee observes, "it is thus clear that Hannah and the wives of their brethren sacrificed equally with their husbands denying the available comforts of life. So it cannot be denied that they were part and parcel of the mission."[70] Hannah's financial contribution to the mission did not remain limited to her thrifty control of the household's budget but extended to a sacrifice of personally generated personal income.

The sudden death of Grant marked only the beginning of constant loss in the Serampore household. In August of 1800, the death of John Fountain left yet another widow--Mary Tidd Fountain--and an infant in Hannah's care. During the year 1801, Daniel Brunsdon and John Thomas died. Joy interrupted their tragedies when, in 1802, William Ward married Fountain's widow. Mary became a steady source of domestic support to Hannah in running the mission household, especially during Hannah's many months of pregnancy.[71] In 1807, Dorothy Carey (1756–1807) died after many years of mental illness and William Carey remarried in 1808. His second wife, Charlotte Rumohr (1761–1821), died in 1821. The following year Carey married for a third time to Grace Hughes (1777–c.1855), who outlived her husband's passing in 1834.

After Hannah's return from England in 1822, the mission family suffered a series of significant personal losses. This difficult period was marked by the tragic deaths of children, children-in-law, grandchildren, and William Ward. At the same time, the mission also suffered a devastating destruction of property by flood and other severe illnesses and accidents among their number. In 1837, Joshua Marshman died, and their son, Benjamin (1802–1838), who

---

[68] Marshman, *Life and Times*, 1:79.

[69] Voigt, "Memoir of Mrs. Hannah Marshman's Earlier Years," 42–45; Chatterjee, *Hannah Marshman*, 41.

[70] Chatterjee, *Hannah Marshman*, 55.

[71] In a conversation with the author on October 19, 2022, Peter DeVires (attendant to the Serampore College archives) indicated that Mary Ward's handwriting often appears in the mission household ledgers during periods coinciding with Hannah's pregnancies.

joined the Chinese class in Serampore by the age of six, died a year later. Hannah and the entire Serampore family walked a path lined with calamity. George Smith commented that Hannah was "a sturdy pillar of support to her family of six, to William Carey's turbulent family, to a series of missionary widows and to many orphans (both native and missionary) over dozens of years, she managed scores of domestic servants from many castes and organized elementary schools for native girls."[72] The Moravian-style mission which Carey envisioned reached beyond their domestic situation. All were called upon to participate in ministry, Hannah prominent among them.

The Mission's work

As the mission work fluctuated, the Serampore missionaries formed an agreement to help guide their domestic and missional lives. As work and life continued, the mission family fell into a natural division of labor yet did not remain rigid in their individual tasks when circumstances demanded a change in the team dynamic. In October of 1805, the brethren of the Serampore Mission produced the *Form of Agreement*, outlining their agreed-upon principles of operation in eleven points, described as "their duty to act in the work of instructing the Heathen."[73] First, they committed to remember the invaluable worth of souls. Second, they would strive to discern obstacles to gospel understanding. Third, they would refrain from attacking beliefs that prejudice the Hindu mind against the gospel when possible. Fourth, they would look for all opportunities to do good. Fifth, they would focus their teaching on Christ's death and sufficiency for conversion. Sixth, in Christian activities, they committed to treating natives as equals. Seventh, they acknowledged the need to disciple and care for converts. Eighth, they would strive to develop Indians as preachers. Ninth, they would engage in the translation of the Bible. Tenth, they committed to steadfast personal prayer and spiritual disciplines. Finally, they promised to give themselves entirely and without limit to the cause. Although the *Agreement* fell to the side in their daily operations, the heart of its content remained at the center of the original missionaries' commitment to the tasks before them.

The work of the Serampore Mission involved numerous activities centred primarily around preaching the gospel, translation, publication, and education. These overarching avenues of ministry provided a general structure and philosophy for the mission. As its ministry methodology evolved toward a greater focus on preparing Indians for the forefront of evangelising, the missionaries took on more of a support role. However, the mission's philosophy remained

---

[72] A. Christopher Smith, "Joshua (1768–1837) and Hannah Marshman (1767–1847)" in *The British Particular Baptists, 1638–1910*, ed. Michael A.G. Haykin (Springfield, MO: Particular Baptist Press, 2000), 2:251.

[73] George Smith, *The Life of William Carey, D. D. Shoemaker and Missionary* (London: John Murray, 1885), 441–450.

centred on a fixed point--to win India for Christ. The initial activities of the missionaries included direct evangelisation of as many natives as possible. The *Agreement* highlights a shift in the missionaries' understanding and a commitment to continue personal preaching of the gospel and Bible translation while also developing education systems for native preachers.[74] An emphasis on the role of education at the core of the mission's methodology grew over time to become one of the key channels for winning India for Christ. Their efforts evidence this both in time spent and finances consumed. This focus led to a multitude of educational efforts by the mission, the most influential of which were its system of public education in the vernacular and the establishment of Serampore College in 1818.[75] As a result of their focused efforts, the Serampore Mission can boast of translating and publishing the first editions of the New Testament in more than thirty languages and dialects.[76] They were the first to hold fast to their conviction to reject caste within the Christian community.[77] The Mission also generated the first native schools for "heathen" children in northern India, the first college for native "catechists and itinerants," and the first native Indian newspaper and religious periodical.[78] The Serampore Mission produced many "firsts," primary among the categories of firsts is their education initiatives.

Each of the central ministry channels demanded a significant amount of financial supports. The BMS provided a base of support for the mission. However, provision for the need beyond finances arriving from England came primarily from revenue through the mission's local ministry efforts. The mission's labours performing this double duty included the Marshmans' boarding schools, Ward's printing press, and Carey's work at Fort William College. J.T. Gracey describes the generosity of the Serampore Mission members, stating that "the one woman [Hannah] and the three men [Carey, Marshman, and Ward], with the children and assistants, were the means of earning nearly half a million dollars for the work of God from the Persian Gulf to the Pacific Ocean … the woman, Hannah Marshman, gave at least one fourth, or more than one hundred thousand dollars."[79] Hannah's financial contribution alone gives evidence to her integral place among the Serampore missionaries.

---

[74] Smith, *Life of William Carey*, 446–449.

[75] Joe L. Coker, "Developing a Theory of Missions in Serampore," *Mission Studies* 18.1/2 (2001): 49.

[76] Marshman, *Life and Times*, 2:523.

[77] Marshman, *Life and Times*, 2:523; A. Christopher Smith, *The Serampore Mission Enterprise* (Bangalore: Centre for Contemporary Christianity, 2006), 144–149.

[78] Marshman, *Life and Times*, 2:523.

[79] J.T. Gracey, *Eminent Missionary Women* (New York: Eaton & Mains, 1898), 155.

Education and the Mission
Hannah's motherly charge of the mission family and her financial contributions to the work evidence only two aspects of Hannah's place on the mission team. As previously stated, education became indispensable to the fulfillment of the Mission's hopes to disseminate the gospel throughout India. In an August 1804 journal entry, Hannah writes:

> Felt some encouragement in reading part of Miss Neale's work, where she had been talking to a child about the Saviour. This I endeavour to do with the children under my care, according to my ability, by explaining the word, by exhorting, admonishing, and striving to bring them to Christ, but the meanness and sinfulness of the instrument often makes me fear that I shall be a cast-away, and they be saved. Oh may they and I be permitted to enter where Jesus is![80]

Hannah's words reflect her vision for the boarding schools. In a letter to a friend, Hannah writes:

> I searched my mind very minutely before I engaged in the School, lest it should be irksome to me afterwards. However I was enabled to leave all, and thankfully to give myself up to the work; and through mercy I have not repented, and hope I never may. I am not worthy of being employed in anything belonging to Christ, and often wonder at the dispensations of God in sending me to this land, where so much grace is needed, and my daily experience is such that I often fear least I have none. This however I know, I long for the increase of Christ's kingdom upon earth, especially in this benighted part of it.[81]

A deep desire to be used by Christ—both personally and in preparing her students for the same—permeated Hannah's labours. Hannah's boarding schools for Eurasian children quickly proved to be successful, generating valuable income for the mission, and bolstering their reputation within the European community. By the end of 1800, the schools proved most successful and contributed a healthy sum of three hundred rupees per month to the mission's purse, eventually becoming a bulwark of income for the mission.[82] As Han-

---

[80] Voigt, "Memoir of Mrs. Hannah Marshman's Earlier Years," 48.

[81] Voigt, "Memoir of Mrs. Hannah Marshman's Earlier Years," 29.

[82] Coker, "Developing a Theory of Missions," 47; Smith, *Serampore Mission Enterprise*, 34, 326; Chatter-

nah's schools increased, they necessitated the property's expansion to house the growing schools.[83] While other members of the mission remained involved in the schools, it was Hannah who managed their funds and expenses.

The educational plans of the Serampore missionaries continued to swell. In 1802, they developed a plan to educate the children of native Christians and the missionary children.[84] In 1807, the mission opened a notable school for native boys.[85] Although Hannah desired to open schools for native girls, this project was delayed due to great prejudice and skepticism of its motives for the fate of the children.[86] M.A. Laird suggests that the greatest success of their educational initiatives came with the founding of the Benevolent Institution in 1809–1810.[87] The institution in Calcutta opened as a charity school for the children of European fathers and native mothers, a segment of society long neglected.[88] Chatterjee rightly notes that Hannah had no direct hand in establishing this institution—as it was not located at Serampore—but likely offered helpful input for its inception.[89] During the years 1819–1824, Hannah developed her Serampore Native Female Education Society.[90] Finally, in 1825, Serampore opened its first school for native females and subsequent projects include an unprecedented school for native adult females.[91]

Hannah's drive to prove the lives of females in Bengal through education

---

jee, *Hannah Marshman*, 44.

[83] Sutapa Dutta, *British Women Missionaries in Bengal, 1793–1861* (London: Anthem, 2017), 67.

[84] Marshman, *Life and Times*, 1:160–161, 164–165.

[85] George Smith, *Twelve Pioneer Missionaries* (London: Thomas Nelson and Sons, 1900), 76.

[86] Chatterjee, *Hannah Marshman*, 45; Dutta, *British Women Missionaries in Bengal*, 74; Caroline Atwater Mason, *Lux Christi: An Outline Study of India* (Norwood: Norwood, 1902), 96. Mason's study of India notes a persistence in the prevention of female education. Mason writes, "so deep is the prejudice against the movement for the education of women that the recent severe droughts have been ascribed to the displeasure of the gods on this account. It has been a popular belief among high-caste women that their husbands would die if they should even learn to read or write" (Mason, *Lux Christi*, 96). The introduction of female education provided a starting point for reversing the trend. However, the Serampore missionaries knew that combatting the underlying issues of dark superstitions and prejudices alone would not change the plight of women in India.

[87] M.A. Laird, "The Contribution of the Serampore Missionaries to Education in Bengal, 1793–1837," *Bulletin of the School of Oriental and African Studies, University of London* 31.1 (1968): 95.

[88] Marshman, *Life and Times*, 1:422–426; Dutta, *British Women Missionaries in Bengal*, 76; Chatterjee, *Hannah Marshman*, 84.

[89] Chatterjee, *Hannah Marshman*, 84.

[90] Smith, *Twelve Pioneer Missionaries*, 76.

[91] Smith, *Twelve Pioneer Missionaries*, 76.

singles her out as the first among her contemporaries. Hannah's boarding school for Eurasian girls at Serampore appear as a first in Bengal.[92] Chatterjee claims that Hannah was the first European woman to join in dispensing education in India and that "the Baptists in Bengal and in England took the lead in launching a strong movement in favour of establishing schools for native girls"—later beginning the "Female Juvenile Society for the establishment and support of Bengali Female Schools."[93] The Serampore Mission experienced only minimal success in these schools. However, Chatterjee notes, "in the history of female education in India particularly in Bengal, the contributions of Hannah Marshman and the Serampore missionaries cannot be underestimated."[94] While other societies developed educational institutions for females, they remained primarily within cities. However, the Serampore Mission stations influenced female education in the villages outside of Calcutta.[95] Additionally, throughout her time in Serampore, Hannah personally encouraged native women and girls to obtain some level of education, and the Serampore Mission schools unofficially allowed some girls attendance.[96] The mission's 1829 report indicates fifteen station schools averaging total attendance of close to one thousand students and female schools with more than six hundred students under the direction of the Serampore Mission.[97] By 1835, they reported seventeen village schools with an average of over one thousand students.[98] Each of these institutions and efforts does not carry the moniker of "Hannah's." However, there is little doubt that her influence—particularly through the immense success of the first Serampore schools—is woven throughout the fabric of the educational efforts flowing from the Serampore Mission.

Shifting responsibilities

The Serampore Mission experienced constant change in many spheres, not

---

[92] Smith, *Twelve Pioneer Missionaries*, 74; Chatterjee, *Hannah Marshman*, 82.

[93] Chatterjee, *Hannah Marshman*, 82, 85; Dutta, *British Women Missionaries in Bengal*, 76–77. Sutapa Dutta explains the development of these efforts as beginning with the Benevolent Christian School Society (est. 1809) opening a free school for boys in Calcutta (1810), then for girls (1811). Dutta states that the Calcutta Baptist Missionary Society—the breakaway society established by the younger missionaries previously attached to Serampore—initiated female education in India, eventually participating in the formation of The Calcutta Female Juvenile Society for the Education of Native Females in 1819.

[94] Chatterjee, *Hannah Marshman*, 90–91.

[95] Chatterjee, *Hannah Marshman*, 90.

[96] Chatterjee, *Hannah Marshman*, 84–85.

[97] Marshman, *Life and Times*, 2:398.

[98] Laird, "Contribution of the Serampore Missionaries to Education in Bengal," 103–104.

limited to death and illness. Political change, evangelistic itineration, mission expansion, and internal controversy all marked the tenure of the original mission members. As the longest-living founding member at Serampore, Hannah weathered the constant change in her circumstances and responsibilities until her last days at Serampore. In April 1801, Carey accepted an appointment to the Fort William College in Calcutta that required him to reside away from Serampore for a majority of the week. For a time, Carey's absence placed a greater burden upon Hannah as she took on the care of Carey's four boys and his insane wife.[99] Even though Carey's second wife intellectually matched her mission family members, she suffered a physical impairment that rendered her an invalid and limited her ability to fully care for the Carey children. While the Marshmans ran the schools at Serampore together, Joshua's absences from Serampore on mission business left Hannah in charge. In 1802, the men commenced itinerating tours out from Serampore. John Clark Marshman records three extended evangelistic visits to Jessore by his father during 1802 and 1803 alone.[100] Hannah shouldered higher levels of responsibility in his absence, specifically in running the schools. In a letter to Andrew Fuller (1754–1815), Joshua explained: "my dear partner [Hannah] is very happy in her employ, although the school, together with the case of her family, and learning Bengali, for which her desire is scarcely less ardent than my own, render her life very laborious."[101] Joshua also travelled to Europe, first in 1822, to meet in person with the BMS committee and again in 1826 for the promotion of funds for Serampore College. During his second visit to Europe (1826–1829), besides bearing increased responsibilities, Hannah also experienced greater turmoil due to the BMS' prolonged internal conflict.

After Hannah suffered the deaths of more children and the devastating fire of the Serampore press in 1812, the surmounting internal controversy consumed much of the correspondence between England and Bengal. New BMS missionaries continued to arrive. Unfortunately, profound differences leading to a years-long painful conflict erupted between the older and younger generations and flowed back and forth across the pond between India and England. In his record of 1808, John Clark Marshman describes the internal state of the Serampore Mission as one of "conflicting dispositions."[102] In Serampore, the heart of the issue seemed to lie in the "rigid self-denial" in which the older missionary families conducted life and to which they expected new

---

[99] Chatterjee, *Hannah Marshman*, 47.

[100] Marshman, *Life and Times*, 1:152–153, 171–174, 184, 188–189. Jessore is located approximately 140 kilometres northeast of Serampore in modern-day Bangladesh.

[101] Chatterjee, *Hannah Marshman*, 50.

[102] "The Late Mr. J. C. Marshman," 401.

missionaries to conform.[103] Coupled with the hardships of operating in a political environment hostile toward missionary endeavors, the differences of opinion and lifestyle forced the cracks in unity to widen. By 1812, the home committee of the BMS had added nineteen new members. Since none of them had had prior personal acquaintance with the original Serampore missionaries, this would have potentially furthered the distance between England and the original Serampore mission. Then, in 1817, five younger missionaries—among them, Carey's nephew, Eustace Carey—broke with the older set at Serampore to form their own mission station in Calcutta. The new mission operated independently from the Serampore Mission yet performed many similar tasks. The Marshmans, particularly Joshua, became the target of attack in the erupting controversy.[104] In 1827 John Clark Marshman notes that "the passions which had hitherto been under some kind of restraint, were now let loose against the Serampore missionaries, and against Dr. Marshman in particular."[105] A friend in Norwich wrote to Joshua in 1828, "Your character lies bleeding in every part of the country."[106] By 1830, the Marshmans felt it necessary to abandon their home within the mission premises. Leaving behind thirty years of memories created in the mission house, the Marshmans relocated to a small house on nearby property they had purchased twelve years prior. Hannah laments leaving so dear a place where eight children and three grandchildren were born.[107] However, this transfer of the mission deeds brought resolution to a portion of

---

[103] Marshman, *Life and Times*, 1:401.

[104] "After the death of the Trio's home committee confidant, Andrew Fuller, in 1815, communication and trust issues forced themselves to the forefront of the Serampore Mission, erupting in a fracture separating the missionaries in residence. The veterans remained in Serampore, and the younger missionaries established a mission base in Calcutta. The questions garnering much attention included who bore proper ownership of the missionaries' locally-generated funds, who held the rights to the Serampore property, and the appropriate level of missionary independence from the home committee. A complete treatment of the controversy is beyond the scope of this essay, yet its presence cannot be discounted in consideration of Hannah's life. For details, see Joseph Ivimey, *Letters on the Serampore Controversy, addressed to the Rev. Christopher Anderson; Occasioned by a Postscript, Dated Edinburgh, 26th November 1830, Affixed to the "Reply" of the Rev. Dr. Marshman* (London, 1831).

[105] Marshman, *Life and Times*, 2:370–371.

[106] Marshman, *Life and Times*, 2:375.

[107] Marshman, *Life and Times*, 2:437, 439. Marshman explained: "by this deed, all the premises were transferred from Dr. Carey and Dr. Marshman, to eleven trustees in England, with the stipulation that they should continue to occupy them rent free during their lives, and that their colleagues should remove from them within three years after the death of the survivor, paying rent intermediately, which was to be made over to the Society, to whom the rents of the premises subsequently were to belong" (Marshman, *Life and Times*, 2:439).

the sixteen-year conflict.[108]

Chatterjee claims that Hannah "calmly ignored all adverse criticisms against them and devotedly continued wholehearted labour for the Mission."[109] One of the hurtful criticisms laid against the Marshmans involved the education of their own children. Because their children attended the mission school, they received the benefits of excellent education and extracurricular activities provided through the school. However, this was reported as the Marshmans devoting extraordinary favour to their own children.[110] While this perception arose out of an imbalanced understanding of the educational system at Serampore and for the missionary children, it must also be recognised that Hannah never received official recognition as a missionary of the BMS. Therefore, the BMS should have had no claim on her personal activities and income.

Hannah's other roles

On the fifth anniversary of their arrival in India, Hannah recalled the blessings of the Lord upon them and opened a candid window into the domestic life of the mission. In the contents of her letter to a Mrs. Clark in Bristol, Hannah lamented the change in her availability for ministry outside the mission's borders. She wrote: "the first three or four months after I came to this country, I had a little time to go out and see the natives … [but since then] my time has been so completely filled up, that sometimes for a month together, I do not go to the extent of our garden."[111] Chatterjee claims that in addition to visiting local women when she was able, "Hannah also acted as counselor and helper to her husband's preaching work."[112] Hannah lived life as a busy woman.

Hannah's maternal charge did not remain limited to those among their mission family and the local community of Serampore. Voigt's memoir records the convalescence and care at the mission home for an ill European woman in Calcutta. The encounter exemplifies how the mission family—with Hannah serving as its mother—received entreaties from the surrounding local and European communities for help. The sick lady featured in Voigt's account convalesced for a time at Serampore and continued to receive care through correspondence and visits upon her return to Calcutta.[113] The mission became a refuge for the

---

[108] Marshman, *Life and Times*, 2:439.

[109] Chatterjee, *Hannah Marshman*, 68.

[110] *Letters Official and Private from the Rev. Dr. Carey* ([London], 1828), 8.

[111] Voigt, "Memoir of Mrs. Hannah Marshman's Earlier Years," 44.

[112] Chatterjee, *Hannah Marshman*, 45.

[113] Voigt, "Memoir of Mrs. Hannah Marshman's Earlier Years," 25–26; Chatterjee, *Hannah Marshman*, 43.

care of widows and orphans. They even set aside a portion of their funds to support widows and orphans.[114]

Hannah's health remained a constant battle during her life. In a January 1801 journal entry, Joshua voiced deep concern over the frequency and severity of Hannah's health problems.[115] In 1820, Hannah returned to England seeking relief from her twenty-year health struggle. However, seeking an improvement in health did not monopolise Hannah's furlough. Chatterjee lists three additional purposes for Hannah's visit to England.[116] First, Hannah sought to set the record straight among friends and relatives regarding their reputations, which had taken severe hits due to the conflict with the young missionaries and the home society. Second, she intended to connect and seek understanding with the new leadership of the BMS. Third, Hannah set out to publicise the work of the Serampore Mission and raise needed support. During her time in England, Hannah learned of the development of a native girls' school in Calcutta and, thus, began a campaign of her own to officially set up a school for native girls.[117]

Hannah remained intimately involved in her husband's missionary efforts and the entire Serampore Mission enterprise. Through all the victories and hardships, Hannah remained a stalwart example of a missionary wife and a missionary in her own right. John Clark Marshman describes his mother as "a woman of feeling, piety, and good sense, of strong mind and great disinterestedness, fitted in every respect to be an associate in the great undertaking to which the life of her husband was devoted, and withal of so amiable a disposition that nothing was ever known to have ruffled her temper."[118] At Hannah's funeral, W.H. Denham (d. 1858) proclaimed: "one feature in our dear friend's character must not be omitted: in fact it characterized the whole period from her illness to her departure—I mean the spirit of prayer."[119] Upon her deathbed, Hannah entreated Denham that "should you say anything to the people about me, after my removal, speak from those words which have been made so precious to me: 'He sent from above, he took me and drew me out of many waters:' but read where Christian [in *The Pilgrim's Progress* by John Bunyan] passes the river."[120] Hannah, thus, became the last living member of the original

---

[114] Marshman, *Life and Times*, 2:425.

[115] Chatterjee, *Hannah Marshman*, 45.

[116] Chatterjee, *Hannah Marshman*, 75.

[117] Chatterjee, *Hannah Marshman*, 75.

[118] Marshman, *Life and Times*, 1:106.

[119] Denham, "Memoir of Mrs. Marshman," 480.

[120] Denham, "Memoir of Mrs. Marshman," 481.

Serampore adults who instituted the mission in 1800. Hannah died on March 5, 1847.

Conclusion

Hannah Marshman dedicated forty-seven years to the work to see all India converted to Christ. More intimately, she gave herself and her family to the founding and cause of the BMS mission station at Serampore and contributed significantly to the ground-breaking work flowing out of the mission. Although the BMS has not recognised her as an official missionary, Hannah's service and dedication demonstrate her rightful place alongside William Carey, William Ward, and her beloved Joshua Marshman in the original Serampore missionary team. Although their personal contributions to the mission effort varied, each devoted invaluable efforts that paved the way for the widespread influence of the Serampore Mission. The words of her adoring husband summarise Hannah's life best. In a deathbed letter from Joshua to Hannah, he wrote: "you have been even to me the best of wives … and you have more than deserved all my love, you have been my strength … in all my trials."[121]

---

[121] Dutta, *British Women Missionaries in Bengal*, 72.

"I have a much larger room to sleep in, and good closets for my books": A study of Joseph Kinghorn's library catalogue

Baiyu Andrew Song

Baiyu Andrew Song FRAS, is the assistant professor of general education studies at Heritage College and Seminary, Cambridge, ON, and an adjunct lecturer at Redeemer University, Ancaster, ON.

On April 20, 1795, Joseph Kinghorn (1766–1832), the young minister of the St. Mary's Baptist congregation in Norwich, wrote to his father David Kinghorn (1737–1822), a fellow Baptist pastor at Bishop Burton, Yorkshire.[1] After a folio-length discussion of theological issues, the son passionately told his father about his new acquisition:

> I have received a parcel of Books from Hamburg lately which are now binding, from which I expect a great deal of pleasure & information. I was somewhat afraid the French should have laid hold on them & to them they wd. have been useless. The most important is Venema's Ecclesiastical History in 7. 4 to Volumes. I had seen a Vol or 2 before I sent for it and I expect I have got a treasure. I have also got a curious Hebrew Bible which I much wanted, for mine is very incorrect. One disadvantage attends it which is the type is small though very distinct. They

---

[1] On David Kinghorn, see Baiyu Andrew Song, "David Kinghorn, 1737–1822" in *The British Particular Baptists, Volume V. More Biographical Essays of Notable British Particular Baptists*, ed. Michael A.G. Haykin and Terry Wolever (Springfield, MO: Particular Baptist Press, 2019), 5:152–175. Also see Martin Hood Wilkin, *Joseph Kinghorn, of Norwich* (Norwich: Fletcher and Alexander, 1855).

were frozen up a long time at Hamburg—and I assure you I was no little pleased when my Cargo arrived safe. In addition to these I sent for a German Edition of a Latin book published about 30 years ago, by Dr. Lowth which was enriched abroad by a great many notes I consequently more valuable than the English printed Edition.—You'll laugh at me I know for all this joy about the new books—but you know one never minds a joke when they have got their wish.[2]

Besides the new Hebrew Bible, the two other titles Kinghorn referred to were Dutch theologian Herman Venema's (1697–1787) *Instituiones Historiae Ecclesiae Veteris et Novi Testamenti*, published from 1777 to 1783 in Leiden (under its Latin name, Lugdunum Batavorum), and Bishop Robert Lowth's (1710–1787), *De Sacra Poesi Hebraeorum*, which was edited by the Prussian philologist Johann David Michaelis (1717–1791) in 1770.[3]

Though Kinghorn had only been the minister of St. Mary's for five years when he wrote this letter, he had already obtained an extensive personal library. When Joseph Kinghorn died in September 1832, Simon Wilkin (1790–1862), Kinghorn's former ward and a designated executor of Kinghorn's properties, quickly drafted a catalogue of the deceased's library, listing every object and book the former owned.[4] Though Wilkin listed 1,514 volumes in Kinghorn's library, a careful study of the catalogue reveals that Wilkin's number was far from being accurate. Since the catalogue was produced in a rush, Wilkin had made various mistakes. For instance, instead of listing every title on the shelves, Wilkin only briefly described bounded volumes of sermons and pamphlets. On other occasions, Wilkin either incorrectly numbered entries, or erroneously recorded book titles.[5] After re-editing Wilkin's catalogue, the number of titles

---

[2] Joseph Kinghorn, Letter to David Kinghorn, April 20, 1795, D/KIN 2/1795 no. 831, Kinghorn Papers (*KPA*) (Angus Library and Archive, Regent's Park College Oxford), 3. Abbreviations in the original text have been expanded to make for easier reading.

[3] Herman Venama, *Institutiones Historiae Ecclesiae Veteris et Novi Testamenti* (Leiden, 1777–1783); Robert Lowth, *De Sacra Poesi Hebraeorum*, ed. Johann David Michaelis (Göttingen, 1770).

[4] Simon Wilkin, ed., *Catalogue of the Entire Library of the Late Rev. Joseph Kinghorn, of Norwich* (Norwich: Wilkin and Fletcher, 1833).

In Joseph Kinghorn's will, Thomas Hawkins (d. 1841) and Simon Wilkin were made the executors ("Will of Reverend Joseph Kinghorn, Dissenting Minister of Norwich, Norfolk," Prerogative Court of Canterbury and Related Probate Jurisdictions: Will Registers, PROB 11/1806/381, Tenterden Quire Numbers: 601–650 [National Archives, Kew]). On Simon Wilkin, see C.B. Jewson, *Simon Wilkin of Norwich* (Norwich, Norfolk: Centre of East Anglian Studies, University of East Anglia, 1979).

[5] For instance, the number 912 is duplicated, as two entries share the same number. Another error occurred to entry 1028, as the number was skipped (see Wilkin, ed., *Catalogue of the Entire Library*, 34). For more editorial errors, see entry 1338. Wilkin recorded: "1338. Vicent's (T.) Explanatory Catechism, 18 mo. 1s. Glasgow, 1750" (Wilkin, ed., *Catalogue of the Entire Library*, 44), however, the correct title for this entry

in Kinghorn's collections came to more than 2,554 in bound volumes and 453 pamphlets and tracts (about 3,007 titles in total), which is significantly impressive for the size of a dissenting minister's personal library.[6] For instance, when Kinghorn was paid to catalogue books in Bristol Academy's library, the Baptist college only had 1,293 titles.[7] Since books were quite expensive, Bristol Academy's library did not grow anywhere near to the size of a modern research library. In 1812, the college had only 2,527 titles (480 titles short of Kinghorn's library).[8] Nevertheless, given the fact that most English Baptist ministers in the

---

is *An Explicatory Catechism*. Another example is entry 1371, where Wilkin recorded: "Wast's (E.) Spiritual Exercises, 18mo. 1s. Glasgow, 1757" (Wilkin, ed., *Catalogue of the Entire Library*, 45), but the correct information is: Elisabeth West, *Memoirs, or, Spiritual Exercises of Elisabeth West; Written by Her Own Hands* (Glasgow, 1757).

[6] The reason for an unclear number is due to entries such as #1310 and #1311, where Wilkin simply recorded "Tracts published by the Society for Promoting Christian Knowledge, a vol. of … 1820," and "[Tracts] of the Society for the Promotion of Permanent and universal Peace, 11 parts in 1 vol. 8vo. and parts … 1831-2" (Wilkin, ed., *Catalogue of the Entire Library*, 43). Although Wilkin has also catalogued all of Kinghorn's pamphlets (some 566 pamphlets), these appear to be unbounded pamphlets (Wilkin, ed., *Catalogue of the Entire Library*, 51-60). Thus, it is impossible to track the total number of bound pamphlets.

For Baptists of this period, useful learning entailed "those several branches of literature in general, which may be serviceable to them, with the blessing of God, in the exercise of their ministry" (Henry Foreman, "The Early Separatists, the Baptists and Education, 1580–1780" [PhD dissertation, Leeds University, 1976], 276; also see Michael A.G. Haykin, "'A Great Thirst for Reading': Andrew Fuller the Theological Reader," *Eusebeia* 9 [2008]: 7-10). Many Baptist ministers thus began to collect books for their private libraries. Though private library records are few and rare, Baptist ministers' libraries were mainly composed of literature written by the Reformers, Puritans, and fellow Baptists. Among the Baptists in the eighteenth century, works by John Gill were essential to read and collect. Baptist minister Abraham Booth's (1734–1806) works were also common. Eighteenth-century ministers also read American authors, and as a result, works by New Divinity theologians like Jonathan Edwards (1703–1758), Joseph Bellamy (1719–1790), Samuel Hopkins (1721–1803), John Smalley (1734–1820), Stephen West (1735–1819), and Jonathan Edwards, Jr. (1745–1801) can also be found in Baptist ministers' libraries. Another feature of the Bristol Baptist Academy's library's collection is Welsh books. By studying a library catalogue of the Academy (1795), Geoffrey F. Nuttall listed thirty-eight titles of Welsh books, which had been collected in the eighteenth century by the Bristol Education Society (Geoffrey F. Nuttall, "Welsh Books at Bristol Baptist College [1795]," *Transactions of the Honourable Society of Cymmrodorion* 9 [2003]: 162–168).

[7] Kinghorn spent two months in 1787 cataloguing every book on the library's shelves. The Bristol Education Society then awarded him £10 for his excellent work. See Joseph Kinghorn, *A Catalogue of the Books in the Library belonging to the Bristol Education Society; In the Order in which they stand on the Shelves. Taken in April & May 1787*, C/01/1787 (Bristol Baptist College).

[8] See Kinghorn, *Catalogue of the Books in the Library belonging to the Bristol Education Society*, C/01/1787 (Bristol Baptist College). Also see Kyle Roberts, "'I have hitherto been entirely upon the borrowing hand': The Acquisition and Circulation of Books in Early Eighteenth-Century Dissenting Academies" in *Print Culture Histories Beyond the Metropolis Account*, ed. James J. Connoly, Patrick Collier, Frank Felsenstein, Kenneth R. Hall, and Robert G. Hall (Toronto, ON: University of Toronto Press, 2016), 54–87; Elizabethaane Boran, "Education and Dissemination of the Word: A Baptist Library in the Eighteenth Century" in *Propagating the Word of Irish Dissent 1650–1800*, ed. Kevin Herlihy (Dublin: Four Courts, 1998), 114–132.

long eighteenth century only had no more than John Gill's (1697–1771) commentaries and his *Body of Divinities*, and a few Puritan works, Bristol Academy's collection was still gigantic. For instance, when Andrew Fuller (1754–1815), the Baptist minister of Kettering and later secretary of the Baptist Missionary Society, compiled a list of all the books in his library on August 28, 1798, there were only 306 titles.[9] Even though Fuller's library was much more extensive than that of the average English Baptist ministers, none of them could compare to Kinghorn's extraordinary library in both number and content.

Being "one of the most learned men" in the Baptist denomination, Joseph Kinghorn's library catalogue provides a glance of Particular Baptist learning at the turning point of denominational institutionalisation.[10] Furthermore, Kinghorn's collections also illustrate how the eighteenth-century Evangelicals were, by default, people of the Enlightenment.

The formation of a library

It is interesting to notice how a dissenting minister like Joseph Kinghorn obtained his massive collections of books. On the one hand, Kinghorn was financially independent. In 1799, when his parents were considering a move to Norwich, Kinghorn told them: "I have £60 in Bank & hope to make it £70 at Lady Day [March 25]. When I have recd. the Legacy it will amount to about £160, this with what you have would form a little annuity for both your lives."[11]

On the cost of books in the eighteenth century, see J.E. Elliott, "The Cost of Reading in Eighteenth-Century Britain: Auction Sale Catalogues and the Cheap Literature Hypothesis," *English Literary History* 77.2 (2010): 353–384; James Raven, "The Book Trades," in *Books and Their Readers in Eighteenth-Century England: New Essays*, ed. Isabel Rivers (London; New York: Continuum, 2001), 1–34.

[9] See *The Diary of Andrew Fuller, 1780–1801*, ed. Michael D. McMullen and Timothy D. Whelan (Berlin: De Gruyter, 2016), 215–236. There is a mistake in Whelan's list. Entry #129 "Hall, Samuel. *Infant-baptism 'from heaven,' and Immersion, as the only mode of Baptism and a Term of Christian Communion, 'of men:' or, A Short Dissertation on Baptism, in Two Parts* (Salem, MA, 1784) is the expanded form of Fuller's abbreviated 'Hall on Infant Bap^{m}'" (*Diary of Andrew Fuller*, ed. McMullen and Whelan, 224). The author was John Cleaveland (1722–1799) and Samuel Hall was the publisher.

[10] Anonymous, "Original Letter of Dr. Ryland," *The Spirit of the Pilgrim* 2.6 (June 1829): 343. On Kinghorn's idea of theological education, see Baiyu Andrew Song, "Joseph Kinghorn's (1766–1832) Educational Vision," *Pacific Journal of Theological Research* 15.1 (May 2020): 23–35.

Such is in strong contrast to Daniel Featley's (1582–1645) criticism of Dissenters, particularly Baptists, as "illiterate Mechanicks," and his warning against these "Schismaticks, and Non-conformists," who "are dunces, and ignorant both Tongues and Arts, they would have no learning, nor Universities" (Daniel Featley, Καταβαπτισται χαταπτυστοι *The Dippers Dipt. Or, the Anabaptists Duck'd and Plung'd over Heave and Eares, at a Disputation in Southwark* [London, 1645], Cc). Regarding criticism over early English Baptists' use of lay or unlearned ministers, see Gordon Kingsley, "Opposition to Early Baptists (1638–1645)," *Baptist History and Heritage* 4.1 (1969): 23–25.

[11] Joseph Kinghorn, Letter to David Kinghorn, January 31, 1799, D/KIN 2/1799 no. 975, *KPA*, 2.

Besides his annual salary, private tutorship, and book royalties, Kinghorn also invested in the stock market, which provided a "considerable interest," though "the stocks are now low, or at least not high."[12] As Kinghorn was never married, after his parents' death, he was financially very well off. His will revealed the Norwich minister's net worth: he owned three properties in Norwich, one on Pottergate Street, one on Bull Close, and one on Thorpe Road.[13] Besides his gift of two hundred pounds to the nonconformist solicitor and later Mayor of Norwich, Thomas Brightwell (1787–1868), Kinghorn also left money for his housemaid Eleanor Cutting, and four Particular Baptist societies, one of which was the Baptist Missionary Society.[14] Thus, besides necessary needs for food and clothes, Kinghorn was able to spend a significant amount of money on books.

On the other hand, it is also intriguing to notice that Kinghorn purchased books from the European continent through friends, such as Thomas Hawkins (d. 1841) and Thomas Theobald (1796–1834)—who were both merchants and members of St. Mary's Baptist Chapel. From their trips to countries like Germany, Hawkins and Theobald brought back news about the religious situation on the Continent and bought requested books for their minister. For instance, when Thomas Theobald went to Leipzig and Hamburg in the autumn of 1797, Kinghorn asked:

> Will you please to procure for me a German & English Dictionary a book of character ... [Johann Gottfried] Eichhorn's [1752–1827] Einleitung ins alten Testament [*Introduction to the Old Testament*] ... [Johann David] Michælis Einleitung d' neuen Bundes [*Introduction to the New Covenant*] ... Michaelis Mosaisches recht [*Mosaic Laws*] ... [Friedrich Gottlieb] Klopstock's [1724–1803] Messiah, an epic poem.[15]

During a time of wars and social instability between Britain and the

---

[12] Joseph Kinghorn, Letter to David Kinghorn, March 19, 1799, D/KIN 2/1799 no. 979, *KPA*, 2.

[13] "Will of Reverend Joseph Kinghorn."

[14] "Will of Reverend Joseph Kinghorn." Thomas Brightwell was the father of English etcher and author Cecilia Lucy Brightwell (1811–1875). Thomas Brightwell had tutored Kinghorn. As he later married Simon Wilkin's sister, Brightwell also became a close friend to Kinghorn. In his will, Kinghorn particularly indicated that the gift was for Cecilia's education. On Thomas Brightwell, see Cecilia Lucy Brightwell, *Memorials of the Life of Mr. Brightwell, of Norwich* (Norwich: Fletcher and Son, 1869).

[15] Joseph Kinghorn, Letter to Thomas Theobald, November 20, 1797, D/KIN 2/1797 no. 933 BCH, *KPA*, 3. Here are the full titles of these books: Johann Gottfried Eichhorn, *Einleitung ins alte Testament und Einleitung ins Neue Testament* (Leipzig, 1811–1824); Johann David Michaelis, *Einleitung in die Gottichen Schriften des Neuen Bundes* (Gottingen, 1788); Michaelis, *Mosaisches Recht* (Frankfort, 1793); Friedrich Gottlieb Klopstock, *Der Messias: Ode an Seine Majestat Frierich den funften, Koning in Danemark und Norvegien* (Halle, 1760).

European continent, Kinghorn was able to purchase books that were unavailable in Britain.

Joseph Kinghorn's library catalogue
When Simon Wilkin drafted Joseph Kinghorn's library catalogue, the former intended to make it a sale catalogue. Thus, besides documenting every item in Kinghorn's library, Wilkin also included a list of books sold at Wilkin and Fletcher bookstore.[16] Structurally, Wilkin's catalogue can be divided into three parts: Kinghorn's mathematical instruments, a list of bound books, and a list of loose pamphlets and sermons.[17] Given their significance, the remainder of this paper will focus on the bound volumes. Kinghorn's library can be divided into a few categories by theme, which are: Patristic literature, Greco-Roman classics, Puritan works, contemporary evangelical writings, theological works on Trinitarianism and Socinianism, scientific works (including mathematics, geography, natural science, and medical science), German and Dutch theological works, journals and magazines, Baptist theology, law and politics, and grammatical references.[18] Without examining each category, this paper highlights a

---

[16] Wilkin, ed., *Catalogue of the Entire Library*, [61–68].

[17] According to Wilkin's catalogue, Kinghorn owned a number of mathematical instruments, including a pair of William Bardin's (fl. 1730–1798) 18-inch globes in stained frames; an Edward Nairne's (1726–1806) patent electrical machine (or electrostatic generator), with cylinder 13 inches by 7, and apparatus; a John Hadley's (1681–1744) quadrant (or octant), in ebony and brass of the best finish, in a box; a hydrostatic balance, in a mahogany box; a George Adams, Jr.'s (1750–1795) universal compound microscope; a John Dollond's (1706–1761) 17-inch achromatic telescope, with 2 1/8-inch aperture, in a shagreen case; a 30-inch refracting telescope; a 15-inch refracting telescope; a box compass, 6-inch diameter; a case of mathematical instruments; an exhausting syringe, with sundry glasses belonging to an air pump; a prism; a land-measuring chain (or Gunter's chain, invented by Edmund Gunter [1581–1626]); a 24-inch box sector, with superior brass joint; parallel and other rules, pocket magnifiers, eye glass, and several reading glasses (Wilkin, ed., *Catalogue of the Entire Library*, [ii]).

On Nairne's electrostatic generator, see Edward Nairne, *The Description and Use of Nairne's Patent Electrical Machine; with the Addition of Some Philosophical Experiments and Medical Observations* (London, 1787). There were also different models of electrostatic generators: a common cylindrical machine with a simple handle; Nairne's; Joseph Priestley's electrifying machine; Read's; Giovanni Battista Beccaria's (1716–1781); Pearson's (David Brewster, *The Edinburgh Encyclopaedia* [Edinburgh, 1830], 8:510–512).

[18] Kinghorn's interest in the church fathers was similar to that of Joseph Priestley (1733–1804). When he met Priestley in early April of 1788, Kinghorn was impressed by the former's scholarship and personality. Kinghorn told his father that the reason for him to study the fathers was "merely because Dr. Priestley takes a good deal of notice of it, and says, amidst all, there are several traces of the opinions of the ancient Christians" (Joseph Kinghorn, Letter to David Kinghorn, November 15, 1791, D/KIN 2/1791 no. 694, *KPA*, 2). In his early pastorate, Kinghorn read "a ponderous tome" written by the Greek and Latin Fathers, "from end to end" (Wilkin, *Joseph Kinghorn*, 450). Also see Joseph Kinghorn's letter to his father David Kinghorn dated November 15, 1791, where Joseph told his father that "I keep doing something with the Fathers though not so much as I could wish the pleasing" (Joseph Kinghorn, Letter to David Kinghorn, November 15, 1791, D/KIN 2/1791 no. 694, *KPA*, 2).

few observations.

German biblical scholarship

Among all Kinghorn's bound volumes, 186 titles are grammatical references, which included dictionaries and concordances in English, Greek, Hebrew, Latin, Arabic, Aramaic, German, Dutch, and French.[19] Kinghorn also owned grammars of both ancient and modern languages. Among these reference works, thirteen were written and edited by Johann Buxtorf, Jr. (1599–1664), a Swiss Protestant Hebraist.[20] Significantly, due to Kinghorn's interest in biblical

---

[19] For instance, Johann Christoph Adelung, *Worterbunch der Hochdeutschen Mundart* (Leipzig, 1793); Robert Ainsworth, *An Abridgement of the Last Quarto Edition of Ainsworth's Dictionary, English and Latin* (London, 1785); Nathan Bailey, *Dictionary English-German and German-English* (Leipzig, 1797); Joseph Baretti (Giuseppe Marc'Antonio Baretti), *An Introduction to the most useful European Languages* (London, 1772); William Bell, *A New Compendious Grammar of the Greek Tongue* (London, 1658); Joannes Christianus Biel, *Novus Thesaurus Philologicus*, ed. E.H. Mutzenbecher (The Hague, 1779); Thomas Boston, *Tractatus Stigmologicus Hebræo-Biblicus: quo accentuum Hebr. doctrina traditur, variusque eorum in explananda S. S. usus exponitur* (Amsterdam, 1738); Carolo Gottlieb Bretschneider, *Lexicon Manvale Greco-Latinvm in Libros Novi Testamenti* (Leipzig, 1824); Marcus Marinus, *Tevat Noah, Arca Noe, sive Thesaurus Linguæ Sanctæ Novus* (Venice, 1593); John Butterworth, *A New Concordance and Dictionary to the Holy Scriptures*, 2nd ed. (Coventry, 1785); Philip Buttmann, *Greek Grammar* (London, 1824); Edmund Castell, *Lexicon Heptaglotton Hebraicum, Chaldaicum, Syriacum, Samaritanum, Aethiopicum, Arabicum, et Persicum* (1669); Nicolas Cleynaerts, קודקדה תוחל *Tabulae in grammaticam Hebraeam* (1555); idem, *Institutiones absolutissimae in linguam Graecam ... multa iam ad codicis emendati fidem sunt restituta* (1582); William Cobbett, *The English Grammar of William Cobbett* (1819); John Pearson, *Critici sacri sive Doctissimorum virorum in SS. biblia annotationes et tractatus* (London, 1660); Gottfried Menthen, *Thesaurus theologico-philologicus, sive Sylloge dissertationum elegantiorum ad selectiora et illustriora Veteris et Novi Testamenti loca* (1701–1702); John Dawson, *Lexicon Novi Testamenti alphabeticum* (1766); John Walker, *A Critical Pronouncing Dictionary and Expositor of the English Language* (London, 1791); Johann Friedrich Fischer, *Dictionarium Breve Chaldædo-Rabbinicum* (Leipzig, 1753); *Encyclopædia Britannica* (Edinburgh, 1797); Thomas Erpenius, *Arabicæ æ linguæ Tyrocinium Id est Thomæ Erpenii Grammatica Arabica* (Leiden, 1656); idem, *Grammatica Arabica cum Fabulis Lokmani* (Leiden, 1767); idem, *Erpenii Arabische Grammatik, abgekürzt, vollständiger und leichter gemacht* (Göttingen, 1771); Erpenius, *Rudimenta Linguæ Arabicæ.* (Leiden, 1770); Heinrich Ewald, *Kristische Grammatik der Hebräischen Sprache* (Leipzig, 1827); August Hermann Francke, *Manuductio ad lectionem scripturae sacrae* (London, 1706); Johann Christoph Gottsched, *Le maitre allemande, ou nouvelle grammaire allemande methodique & raissonnée* (Strasbourg, 1760).

[20] Kinghorn owned the following works of Buxtorf: *Epitome Grammaticæ Hebrææ, Breviter & Methodice ad publicam Scholarum usum proposita* (Leiden, 1716); *Florilegium Hebraicum* (Basel, 1648/9); *De Abbreviaturis Hebraicis, Recensio Talmudi, et Bibliotheca Rabbinica* (Basel, 1640); *Manuale Hebraicum et Chaldaicum* (Basel, 1658); *Lexicon Breve Rabbinico-Philosophicum* (n.d.); *Specimen Phraseologiæ V. T. Hebraicæ* (Frankfurt, 1717); *Lexicon Hebraicum et Chaldaicum* (London, 1646); *Grammaticæ Chaldaicæ et Syriacæ* (Basel, 1650); *Thesaurus Grammaticus Linguæ Hebrææ* (Basel, 1663); *Lexicon Chaldaicum et Syriacum* (Basel, 1622); *Liber Cosri continens Colloquium seu Disputationem de religione* (Basel, 1660); *Dissertationes Philologico-Theologicae* (Basel, 1662); *Tractatus de Punctorum vocalium et accentuum* (Basel, 1648).

On Buxtorf, see Stephen G. Burnett, *From Christian Hebraism to Jewish Studies: Johannes Buxtorf (1564–1629) and Hebrew Learning in the Seventeenth Century* (Leiden: Brill, 1996); Burnett, "Distorted Mirrors: Antonius Margaritha, Johann Buxtorf and Christian Ethnographies of the Jews," *The Sixteenth Century Jour-*

criticism, more than a quarter of his books were written by German philologists and theologians. In particular, Kinghorn owned 24 works written and edited by Johann David Michaelis, who, being influenced by Bishop Robert Lowth, became "concerned with the philological and cultural determinants of the Bible rather than with its theology."[21] Being influenced by Michaelis, Kinghorn investigated the philological and cultural determinants of the biblical texts, yet without wholly rejecting typology, as he saw the New Testament as "the only standard to which we can appeal, respecting the truths of the Gospel Revelation."[22] Besides Michaelis, several German biblical critics' works can also be found in Kinghorn's library. For instance, Johann Jakob Griesbach (1745–1812), Johann Friedrich Wilhelm Jerusalem (1709–1789), Friedrich Adolf Lampe (1683–1729), Heinrich Eberhard Gottlob Paulus (1761–1851), Johann Salomo Semler (1725–1791), Friedrich Spanheim, Jr. (1632–1701), and Gottlob Christian Storr (1736–1805) among others.[23] Most of these authors

---

nal 25.2 (1994): 275–287; Ernst Staehelin, "Der Briefwechsel zwischen Johannes Buxtorf II und Johannes Coccejus," *Theologische Zeitschrift* 4.5 (1948): 372–291; Anthony Grafton, and Joanna Weinberg, "Johann Buxtorf Makes a Notebook," in *Canonical Texts and Scholarly Practices: A Global Comparative Approach*, ed. Anthony Grafton, and Glenn W. Most (Cambridge: Cambridge University Press, 2016), 275–298; Rudolf Smend, *Vier Epitaphe—die Basler Hebraisten—Familie Buxtorf* (Berlin: de Gruyter, 2010); Theodor Dunkelgrün, "The Humanist Discovery of Hebrew Epistolography," in *Jewish Books and Their Readers: Aspects of the Intellectual Life of Christians and Jews in Early Modern Europe*, ed. Scott Mandelbrote, and Joanna Weinberg (Leiden: Brill, 2016), 211–259; Eveline van Staalduine-Sulman, *Justify Christian Aramaism: Editions and Latin Translations of the Targums from the Complutensian to the London Polyglot Bible (1517–1657)* (Leiden: Brill, 2017), 178–180.

[21] Marcus Walsh, "Biblical Scholarship and Literary Criticism," in *The Cambridge History of Literary Criticism. Volume 4 The Eighteenth Century*, ed. H.B. Nisbet and Claude Rawson (Cambridge University Press, 1997), 771.

[22] Joseph Kinghorn, *Scriptural Arguments for the Divinity of Christ* (Norwich, [1814]), iii. Also see Michael C. Legaspi, *The Death of Scripture and the Rise of Biblical Studies* (Oxford: Oxford University Press, 2010).

[23] Johann Jakob Griesbach, *Symbolae criticae ad supplendas et corrigendas variorum N.T. lectionum collectiones* (Halle, 1785); Johann Friedrich Wilhelm Jerusalem, *Betrachtungen über die vornehmsten Wahrheiten der Religion* (Braunschweig, 1776); Friedrich Adolf Lampe, *Synopsis Historiæ Sacræ et Ecclesiasticæ* (Utrecht, 1735); Heinrich Eberhard Gotttlob Paulus, *Philologisch-kritischer und historischer Commentar über das Neue Testament* (Lübeck, 1800); idem, *Zusätze und verbessernde Änderungen aus der zweyten, durchaus verbesserten Ausgabe der drey ersten Theile des philologisch-kritischen und historischen Commentars über das Neue Testament* (Lübeck, 1808); idem, *Philologisch-kritischer und historischer Commentar über das Evangelium des Johannes* (Lübeck, 1804); Johann Salomo Semler, *Paraphrasis in primam Pauli ad Cointhios Epistolam cum notis* (Halle, 1770); idem, *Paraphrasis in Primam Ioannis Epistolam* (Regiae, 1792); idem, *Paraphrasis epistolae Iacobi: cum notis et Latinarum translationum varietate* (Regiae, 1781); idem, *Paraphrasis in epistolam II. Petri, et epistolam Judae* (Regiae, 1784); idem, *Paraphrasis epistolae ad Galatas* (Regiae, 1779); idem, *Commentarii Historici de Antiquo Christianorum statu* (Halle, 1771); Friedrich Spanheim, the younger, *Histoire de la Papesse Jeanne fidèlement tirée de la dissertation Latine* (La Haye, 1720); Gottlob Christian Storr, *Pauli Brief an die Hebræer* (Tübingen, 1809).

were influenced by the Enlightenment and advocated for historical-grammatical and even naturalistic interpretations of the Scriptures. For instance, Johann Jerusalem, the founder of doctrinal criticism, argued that

> dogmas such as the doctrine of the "two natures" and the Trinity were not to be found in the New Testament. If anything, these arose through confusion of the Platonic *logos-concept* with that found in the fourth gospel, and the mistaken apprehension that Jesus personified, rather than exemplified, this *logos*. The history of dogma was thus a history of mistakes.[24]

On the other hand, Johann Salomo Semler has been considered the father of German rationalism, and Heinrich Paulus provided a naturalistic explanation of Jesus' miracles, and proposed "the swoon theory," doubting Jesus' death.[25] It is also interesting to find that Kinghorn owned Johann Gottfried Herder's (1744–1803) *Briefe, das Studium der Theologie betreffend*, and three works by Johann Gottfried Eichhorn. Regarding the latter, it is known that Eichhorn regarded much of the Bible as mere human writings. As a result, Eichhorn argued that biblical scholars ought to develop "a thorough knowledge of [the Bible's] distinctive historical and cultural character" in order to understand the biblical

---

[24] Alister E. McGrath, *Christian Theology: An Introduction*, 5th ed. (Malden, MA; Oxford; Chichester, West Sussex: Wiley-Blackwell, 2011), 297.

[25] On Semler, see Gottfried Hornig, *Johann Salomo Semler: Studien zu Leben und Werk des Hallenser Aufklärungstheologen* (Tübingen: Max Niemeyer Verlag, 1996); Eric Wilhelm Carlsson, "Johann Salomo Semler, the German Enlightenment, and Protestant Theology's Historical Turn" (PhD diss., University of Wisconsin-Madison, 2006); Anders Gerdmar, *Roots of Theological Anti-Semitism: German Biblical Interpretation and the Jews, from Herder and Semler to Kittel and Bultmann* (Leiden: Brill, 2009), 39–50; Eric Carlsson, "Pietism and Enlightenment Theology's Historical Turn: The Case of Johann Salomo Semler," in *The Pietist Impulse in Christianity*, ed. Christian T. Collins Winn, Christopher Gehrz, G. William Carlson, and Eric Holst (Cambridge: James Clarke, 2011), 97–106; Johannes Wischmeyer, "Continuity and Change: The Study of Protestant Theology in Germany between Reformation and the Humboldtian University Ideal," *Communio Viatorum* 47.3 (2005): 240–256; Boris Paschke, "The Contribution of Johann Salomo Semler to the Historical Criticism of the New Testament," *Concordia Theological Quarterly* 80.1-2 (2016): 113–132; Andrew McKenzie-McHarg, "Putting a Positive Spin on Priestcraft. Accommodation and Deception in Late-Enlightenment German Theology," *Intellectual History Review* 28.1 (2018): 201–224.

Paulus proposed that Jesus did not die on the cross; instead, he fell into a temporary coma and revived without help in the tomb. On Paulus, see Henning Graf Reventlow, "Rationalistische Exegese: Am Beispiel des Heinrich Eberhard Gottlieb Paulus (1761–1851)," in *Gottes Recht als Lebensraum: Festschrift für Hans Jochen Boecker*, ed. Peter Mommer (Neukirchen-Vluyn: Neukirchener, 1993), 211–225. Paulus' naturalistic reading of the gospels was partially due to the Unitarian influence he encountered at Cambridge in 1788 (see Ruth Barton, "Miracles," in *The Edinburgh Critical History of Nineteenth-Century Christian Theology*, ed. Daniel Whistler [Edinburgh: Edinburgh University Press, 2018], 148).

texts.²⁶ At the same time, Kinghorn also read works by the Cocceians, a school of thought named after Dutch divine Johannes Cocceius (1603–1669), who in contrast to Gisbertus Voetius (1589–1676), "developed a particular historical, federal, and spiritual Bible exegesis and theology."²⁷ These include works by Friedrich Adolf Lampe, a Calvinistic Pietist and a follower of Johannes d'Outrein (1662–1722), and Fredrich Spanheim, Jr., a German Calvinist.

Although Martin Hood Wilkin stated in his biography of Kinghorn that the latter's theological influence mainly came from Germany, it is interesting to notice that Kinghorn only paid attention to German biblical criticism.²⁸ For instance, Kinghorn did not own any work by Immanuel Kant (1724–1804), Johann Georg Hamann (1730–1788), Georg Wilhelm Friedrich Hegel (1770–1831), or Friedrich Schleiermacher (1768–1834), whose works were not difficult to obtain. Nevertheless, the influence of Johann Lorenz von Mosheim (1693–1755) needs noting.²⁹ Kinghorn owned nine of Mosheim's works, and he consistently told his father about his admiration for Mosheim.³⁰ When King-

---

²⁶ Walsh, "Biblical Scholarship and Literary Criticism," 775.

²⁷ Aza Goudriaan, *Reformed Orthodoxy and Philosophy, 1625-1750: Gisbertus Voetius, Petrus van Mastricht, and Anthonius Driessen* (Leiden: Brill, 2006), 13. On Cocceius, see Willem J. van Asselt, *Johannes Coccejus: Potret van een zeventiende-eeuwse theology op oude en nieuwe wegen* (Heerenveen, 1997); idem, "*Amicitia Dei* as Ultimate Reality: An Outline of the Covenant Theology of Johannes Cocceius (1603–1669)," *Ultimate Reality and Meaning. Interdisciplinary Studies in the Philosophy of Understanding* 21.1 (1998): 35–47; idem, *The Federal Theology of Johannes Cocceius (1602–1660)* (Leiden: Brill, 2001); Brian J. Lee, *Johannes Cocceius and the Exegetical Roots of Federal Theology: Reformation Developments in the Interpretation of Hebrews 7–10* (Göttingen: Vandenhoeck & Ruprecht, 2009); Casey B. Carmichael, *A Continental View: Johannes Cocceius's Federal Theology of the Sabbath* (Göttingen: Vandenhoeck & Ruprecht, 2019).

²⁸ Wilkin, *Joseph Kinghorn*, 429, 449.

²⁹ On Mosheim, see Lewis Spitz, Jr., "Johann Lorenz Mosheim's Philosophy of History," *Concordia Theological Monthly* 20.5 (1949): 321–339; Karl Heussi, *Johann Lorenz Mosheim. Ein Beitrag zur Kirchengeschichte des achtzehnten Jahrhunderts* (Tübingen: Mohr, 1906); E.P. Meijering, *Die Geschichte der christlichen Theologie im Urteil J.L. von Mosheims* (Amsterdam: J.C. Gieben, 1995); Martin Mulsow, Ralph Häfner, Florian Neumann, and Helmut Zedelmaier, eds., *Johann Lorenz Mosheim (1693–1755): Theologie im Spannungsfeld von Philosophie, Philologie und Geschichte* (Wiesbaden: Harrassowitz, 1997).

On Semler, see Trutz Rendtorff, *Church and Theology: The Systematic Function of the Church Concept in Modern Theology*, trans. Reginald H. Fuller (Philadelphia: Westminster, 1971), 28–58; William Baird, *History of New Testament Research Volume One From Deism to Tübingen* (Minneapolis, MN: Fortress, 1992), 117–127; Gottfried Hornig, *Johann Salomo Semler: Studien zu Leben und Wek des Hallenser Aufklärungstheologen* (Berlin: de Gruyter, 1996).

³⁰ These are *Dissertationum ad Historiam Ecclesiasticam* (Altona, 1733); *De Rebus Christianorum ante Constantinum magnum commentarii* (Helmstedt, 1753); *Institutiones Historiae Christianae Majores saeculum primum* (Helmstedt, 1739); *Institutiones Historiae Christianae Antiquioris* (Helmstedt, 1737); *Vindiciae Antiquae Christianorum Disciplinae* (Hamburg, 1722); *Dissertationum ad Sanctiores Disciplinas Pertinentium Syntagma* (Leipzig, 1733); *Elementa Theologiae Dogmaticae in academicis quondam praelectionibus proposita et demonstrata*, ed. Christian Ernst von Windheim (Nuremberg, 1758); *De Beghardis et Beguinabus*

horn first got hold of Mosheim's *Ecclesiastical History* in Latin in December 1791, he told his father: "I am now in possession of a treasure of curious Information which is perhaps the sweeter because very few in the Kingdom are in this respect equally rich."[31] A few months later, Kinghorn told his father:

> I have lately got 6 vols of Mosheims Works principally on Ecclesiastical History. The other parts on Divinity so that I have another pretty long piece of work to unravel his crabbed Latin which I think by no means a model of good writing only it contains valuable information. One of his Volumes is Elementa Theologia Dogmaticæ written with a clearness of idea I have seldom if ever seen. I see on the subject of Election he is an Arminian though I think as near a Calvinist as an Arminian can be.[32]

Later, on October 2, Kinghorn also discussed Mosheim's argument of academies in the Patristic period with his father.[33] Significantly, Mosheim's influence also indirectly caused the debate between Kinghorn and Robert Hall, Jr. (1764–1831) over the terms of communion. Hall embraced Mosheim's Enlightenment historiography and "viewed history in a pragmatic, functionalist, nonsupernaturalist way, distinguished between true religion ('spiritual, moral, free') and church doctrine, construed the church as an association on a par with other human societies such as the state, and stressed the principle of individuality and subjectivity."[34] Kinghorn, on the other hand, upheld an Augustinian view

---

commentaries (Leipzig, 1790); and *An Ecclesiastical History*, trans., Archibald Maclaine (London, 1806). See Wilkin, *Catalogue*, 30. Kinghorn also owned six works by Semler, which are: *Paraphrasis in primam Pauli ad Cointhios Epistolam* (Halle, 1770); *Paraphrasis in Primam Ioannis Epistolam* (Regiae, 1792); *Paraphrasis epistolae Iacobi* (Regiae, 1781); *Paraphrasis in epistolam II. Petri, et epistolam Judae* (Regiae, 1784); *Paraphrasis epistolae ad Galatas* (Regiae, 1779); and *Commentarii Historici de Antiquo Christianorum statu* (Halle, 1771). See Wilkin, *Catalogue*, 39.

[31] Joseph Kinghorn, Letter to David Kinghorn, December 10, 1791, D/KIN 2/1791 no. 701, *KPA*, 3.

[32] Joseph Kinghorn, Letter to David Kinghorn, May 28, 1792, D/KIN 2/1792 no. 720, *KPA*, 2. Abbreviations have been expanded to make for easier reading.

[33] Joseph Kinghorn, Letter to David Kinghorn, October 2, 1792, D/KIN 2/1792 no. 741, *KPA*, 1–2.

[34] Peter C. Hodgson, *Revisioning the Church: Ecclesial Freedom in the New Paradigm* (Philadelphia: Fortress, 1988), 53. Hall rejected the distinction between the visible and invisible church; instead, like many nineteenth-century theologians, he understood the church in terms of its "historical existence" and "ideal essence." For Hall, "we must either seek a church such as it not to be found upon earth, or to be content to associate with men compassed with infirmities; prepared to exercise towards others the forbearance and indulgence which we need, and to exhibit on every occasion the humility becoming those who are conscious that in 'many things we all offend'" (*A Reply to the Rev. Joseph Kinghorn: Being a Further Vindication of the Practice of Free Communion* [Leicester, 1818], 104–105).

of a dualistic nature of the church.³⁵

The Reformed authors

The other main theological influence on Kinghorn are works written by the seventeenth-century Puritans, eighteenth-century Evangelicals, and Dutch Reformed divines. Of the Puritan authors, Kinghorn owned 29 works by John Owen (1616–1683), and 31 works by Richard Baxter (1615–1691).³⁶ As for

---

³⁵ Kinghorn rejected both Donatism and *permixta ecclesia*. Instead, Kinghorn understood paedobaptists as erring Christians, and he distinguished the "Jewish church" from the Christian church. In 1829, when a Norfolk Anglican clergyman published an attack on the Dissenters, Kinghorn quickly responded though anonymously. Following his theological opponent's definition of the church, Kinghorn stated: "Without discussing all the parts of the definition, or enquiring how far they would extend, I will take the last line or two as a common basis, that is church is a body of persons composed of those who are joined together in the 'acknowledgment of *one Lord, one faith, one baptism:*' and I agree with him, that the present enquiry is not concerning the *invisible*, but the visible church, if the terms are properly understood" (*Remarks on a "Country Clergyman's Attempt to Explain the Nature of the Visible Church, the Divine Commission of the Clergy, &c." Being a Defence of Dissenters in General, and of Baptists in Particular; On New Testament Principles* [Norwich: S. Wilkin, 1829], 5).

³⁶ Owen's works included: *Exposition of the Epistles to the Hebrews* (1668–1684); *Exposition of the Epistles to the Hebrews*, rev. and abridged by Edward Williams (London, 1790); *Death of Death in the Death of Christ* (1648); *Reason of faith* (1677); *True nature of schism* (1657); *Thirteen Sermons preached on various occasions* (London, 1756); *Day of Rest* (1671); *Divine Justice*; *Mortification of Sin*; *Temptation* (1817); *Duty of being spiritually-minded* (1816); *Doctrine of Justification by Faith* (Glasgow, 1760); *Apostacy* (1676); *Display of Arminianisme* (1642); *Exposition on the CXXXth Psalm* (Edinburgh, 1798); *Gospel grounds and evidences* (1811); *Doctrine of the saints' perseverance* (Oxford, 1654); *Vindiciae Evangelicae; or, the mystery of the gospel vindicated* (Oxford, 1655); *Original, nature, &c. of Evangelical Churches* (1681); *Indwelling-sin* (1668); *Waies and Means of understanding the mind of God* (1678); *Glorious mystery of the person of Christ* (1679); *The Deity of Christ* (1691); *Communion with God* (Glasgow, 1763); *Guide to Church-Fellowship* (1692); *Discourse concerning the Holy Spirit* (Glasgow, 1791); *Lord's Supper* (Edinburgh,1798); *True Nature of a Gospel Church* (Glasgow, 1801); *De Natura ortu, progressu, et studio Verae theologiae libri* (Oxford, 1661). See Wilkin, *Catalogue*, 83.

The works by Baxter were: *A Key for Catholicks* (London, 1659); *Certain Disputations of Right to Sacraments, and the true nature of Visible Christianity* (London, 1657); *Life of Faith* (London, 1670); *The Cure of Church-divisions* (London, 1670); *The Divine Life* (London, 1664); *A Treatise of Conversion* (London, 1657); *The English Nonconformity*, 2ⁿᵈ ed. (London, 1690); *A Second True Defence of the Meer Nonconformists* (London, 1681); *A Saint or a Brute* (London, 1655); *The Arrogancy of Reason against Divine Revelations, Repressed* (London, 1655); *For Prevention of the unpardonable sin against the Holy-Ghost* (London, 1655); *Plain Scripture Proof of Infants Church-membership and Baptism* (London, 1658); *The Reasons of the Christian Religion* (London, 1667); *A Holy Commonwealth, Or Political Aphorisms, Opening the true Principles of Government* (London, 1692); *Imputative Righteousness Truly Stated, According to the Tenour of the Gospel* (London, 1679); *A Treatise of Justifying Righteousness* (London, 1676); *The Mischiefs of Self-Ignorance, and the Benefits of Self-Acquaintance, Opened in Divers Sermons at Dunstan's-West* (London, 1662); *Universal Redemption of Mankind, by the Lord Jesus Christ: Stated and Cleared by the late Learned Mr. Richard Baxter. Whereunto is added a short Account of Special Redemption, by the same Author* (London, 1694); *The Catechizing of Families* (London, 1683); *The Poor Man's Family Book*, 6ᵗʰ ed. (London, 1697); *The Poor Man's Family Book* (1818 ed.); *Richard Baxter's Dying Thoughts upon Phil. I. 23* (London, 1683); *A Christian Directory* (London, 1673); *The Saints Everlasting Rest*, abridg. Benjamin Fawcett (Salop, 1759); *A Treatise of Episcopacy* (Lon-

evangelical authors, it seems that Jonathan Edwards (1703–1798) and Philip Doddridge (1702–1751) were his favourites, as Kinghorn owned nine works by the American divine, and nine works by the English Congregationalist.[37] Besides English authors, Kinghorn also owned works by Dutch theologians such as Johannes Cocceius, Hugo Grotius (1583–1645), Philippus van Limborch (1633–1712), Salomon van Til (1643–1713), Herman Venema (1697–1787), Campegius Vitringa, Sr. (1659–1722), and Herman Witsius (1636–1708).[38] Specifically, Limborch's *Amica collatio cum erudite Judaeo* (1687) led Kinghorn to emphasize that the Old and New Testaments "should be understood primarily within the context of their time" and the "Christian faith is grounded in the New Testament."[39] However, unlike Limborch, who believed that the person

don, 1681); *Church-History of the Government of Bishops and Their Councils Abbreviated* (London, 1680); *Methodus Theologiæ Christianæ* (London, 1681); *A Paraphrase on the New Testament*, Rev. ed. (London, 1810); *Reliquiæ Baxterianæ*, ed. Matthew Sylvester (London, 1696); Edmund Calamy, ed., *An Abridgement of Mr. Baxter's History of his Life and Times* (London, 1702); *Converse with God in solitude* (London, 1813). See Wilkin, *Catalogue*, 3–4, 48.

[37] Edwards' works were: *The Works of President Edwards, in Eight Volumes* (Leeds, 1806–1811); *Practical Sermons* (Edinburgh, 1788); *Sermons on Various Important Subjects* ([Edinburgh], 1785); *A Faithful Narrative on the Surprizing Work of God*, 2nd ed. (London, 1738); *An Essay on the Nature of True Virtue* (London, 1778); *Twenty Sermons* (Edinburgh, 1789); *Remarks on Important Theological Controversies* (Edinburgh, 1796); *A Treatise Concerning Religious Affections* (London, 1762); Samuel Hopkins, *The Life and Character of the late Reverend, Learned, and Pious Mr. Jonathan Edwards ... And also, Eighteen Select Sermons on Various Important Subjects* (Glasgow, 1785). See Wilkin, *Catalogue*, 15.

The works by Doddridge were: *Sermons to Young Persons* (London, 1735); *A Course of Lectures on the Principal Subjects in Pneumatology, Ethics, and Divinity*, 2nd ed. (London, 1776); *Lectures on Preaching* (London, 1807); *Hymns*, ed. Job Orton (Salop, 1755); *Hymns* (1811); *The Works of the Rev. P. Doddridge, D.D. In Ten Volumes* (Leeds, 1802–1804). See Wilkin, *Catalogue*, 14.

[38] See Aaron L. Katchen, *Christian Hebraists and Dutch Rabbis: Seventeenth Century Apologetics and the Study of Maimonides' Misneh Torah* (Cambridge, MA: Harvard University Press, 1984); Adriaan C. Neele, *Before Jonathan Edwards: Sources of New England Theology* (Oxford: Oxford University Press, 2019).

[39] Philippus van Limborch, *De Veritate Religionis Christianae Amica Collatio cum Erudite Judeo* (Gouda, 1687). It appears that Kinghorn obtained a copy of Limborch's book in the first few weeks of 1797, as he wrote to his father: "Lately I have not with a book for wc. I have been on the look out some years without being able to obtain a sight of it—Now it is mine. It is Limborch's Amica collatis cum Judæa erudio. The controversy was carried on the writing & each party explained his sentiments & the arguments on wc. they were built. I have not read much of it yet for it has only been mine a few days—but I expect much information from it" (Joseph Kinghorn, Letter to David Kinghorn, January 17, 1797, D/KIN 2/1797 no. 896, *KPA*, 2). On Limborch, also see J.V. Fesko, *The Covenant of Works: The Origins, Development, and Reception of the Doctrine* (Oxford: Oxford University Press, 2020), 119–136; Kęstutis Daugirdas, "The Biblical Hermeneutics of Philip van Limborch (1633–1712) and its Intellectual Challenges" in *Scriptural Authority and Biblical Criticism in the Dutch Golden Age: God's World Questioned*, ed. Dirk van Miert, Henk Nellen, Piet Steenbakkers, and Jetze Touber (Oxford: Oxford University Press, 2017), 219–239; J.V. Fesko, *The Covenant of Redemption: Origin, Development, and Reception* (Göttingen: Vandenhoeck & Ruprecht, 2015); Mark A. Herzer, "Adam's Reward: Heaven or Earth?," in *Drawn into Controversie: Reformed Theological Diversity and Debates Within Seventeenth-Century British Puritanism*, ed. Michael A.G. Haykin and Mark Jones (Göttingen: Vandenhoeck

of Jesus Christ could only be defended from the New Testament, Kinghorn believed the completeness of the divine revelation in the Old and New Testaments. Though Kinghorn followed Limborch's method, Kinghorn emphasized the need to read the Old Testament Christologically or typologically.

Other works
Theologically, Kinghorn was especially interested in the controversies on the doctrines of the Trinity and the sacraments. Specifically, Kinghorn owned works written on both sides of the Trinitarian controversy in the seventeenth and eighteenth centuries.[40] He also owned works written by Roman Catholic theologians.[41] Besides theological subjects, Kinghorn also read books in natural science, mathematics, and astronomy. He owned more than fifty titles on natural and medical science in his library. For instance, he owned Henry Baker's (1698–1774), *The Microscope Made Easy*; Henry Bickersteth, Baron Langdale's (1781–1851), *Medical Hints, designed for the use of Clergymen*; and George Cheyne's (1672–1743), *Philosophical Principles of Natural Religion*.[42] Kinghorn, like many eighteenth-century Evangelicals, lived in the transition from "natural philosophy to the natural sciences."[43]

Conclusion
Joseph Kinghorn's library is unique. Kinghorn's interest in textual criticism, rabbinical literature, hermeneutics, and philology gave his library a far more academic quality than that of Andrew Fuller.[44] And in contrast to the Bristol Academy's library, Kinghorn's was filled with German, Dutch, and French theological works. The catalogue also reveals his broad interest in the knowledge of

---

& Ruprecht, 2011), 162–182; Jeremy F. Worthen, *The Internal Foe: Judaism and Anti-Judaism in the Shaping of Christian Theology* (Newcastle upon Tyne: Cambridge Scholars Publishing, 2009); Luisa Simonutti, "Limborch's *Historia Inquisitionis* and the Pursuit of Toleration" in *Judaeo-Christian Intellectual Culture in the Seventeenth Century: A Celbration of the Library of Narcissus Marsh (1638-1713)*, ed. Allison P. Coudert, Sarah Hutton, Richard H. Popkin, and Gordon M. Weiner (Dordrecht, the Netherlands: Kluwer, 1999), 237–256; T. Marius van Leeuwen, "Philippus van Limborch's *Amica Collatio* and its Relation to Grotius's *De Veritate*," *Grotiana* 35.1 (2014): 163.

[40] For instance, see Wilkin, *Catalogue*, 23, 45–47.

[41] For instance, see Wilkin, *Catalogue*, 19, 28.

[42] Wilkin, *Catalogue*, 2, 6, 11.

[43] D. Bruce Hindmarsh, *The Spirit of Early Evangelicalism: True Religion in a Modern World* (Oxford: Oxford University Press, 2018), 106.

[44] In contrast, Kinghorn and Fuller only had 72 titles in common. Most of these titles were written by Baptist leaders such as John Bunyan (1628–1688), John Gill (1697–1771), John Ryland, Jr. (1753–1825), and early evangelicals such as Jonathan Edwards.

various subjects and disciplines. Though the catalogue by itself cannot explain the degree of influence of different works upon Kinghorn's theological formation, it certainly indicates his open-mindedness. Living in the age of Enlightenment and revolutions, Kinghorn embraced the spirit of the age without calling into question his Christian orthodoxy.

Texts & documents

Jane Porter (c.1761–1808) of Bath

ed. Courtney Bachert & introd. Baiyu Andrew Song

Courtney Bachert is a graduating student at Heritage College and Seminary. She is currently working on the project "Baptist Women in the Late Georgian Era" under the supervision of Baiyu Andrew Song.

Baiyu Andrew Song FRAS is the assistant professor of general education studies at Heritage College and Seminary, Cambridge, ON, and an adjunct lecturer at Redeemer University, Ancaster, ON.

Introduction

Baptist women had different experiences in the long eighteenth century. Though women like Anne Dutton (1692–1765) and Anne Steele (1717–1778) published multiple works, they had to defend the legitimacy of their writing ministries.[1] As John Briggs has noticed, while women's contribution to church life was limited, they were active in hymn-writing, education, charities, and oversea missions.[2] Consequently, few Baptist women are known, and fewer of their works are read. Recent scholarship tries to diversify the traditional

---

[1] For instance, see Anne Dutton, *A Letter to Such of the Servants of Christ, Who May Have Any Scruple about the Lawfulness of Printing Any Thing Written by a Women* (London, 1743). Also see Timothy D. Whelan, and Julia Griffin, eds., *Nonconformist Women Writers, 1720–1840* (London: Pickering & Chatto, 2011); Timothy D. Whelan, *Other British Voices: Women, Poetry, and Religion, 1766–1840* (London: Palgrave Macmillan, 2015).

[2] John Briggs, "She-Preachers, Widows and Other Women: The Feminine Dimension in Baptist Life since 1600," *Baptist Quarterly* 31.7 (1986): 337–352.

narrative by focusing on different topics and aspects of the Baptist life experience.[3] Being a part of the "Baptist Women in the Late Georgian Era" project, Courtney Bachert and I are working through the *Baptist Magazine* (1809–1863) and focus on Baptist women's biographies that were published in the late Georgian era (down to the death of George IV in 1830). In the *Baptist Magazine*, most information about the lives of Baptist women can be found in the obituary section. While memoirs of Baptist ministers were featured on the cover page of different issues, selective women's lives were written by either their husbands or friends for spiritual nourishment and memorial in the latter sections of the magazine.

The biography of Jane Porter (c.1761–1808) was the first of these women's biographies to appear in the *Baptist Magazine*. Little is known about her life besides the following text. Curiously, in Philip Cater's biography of John Paul Porter (1759–1832), Jane's husband, the biographer did not record much about Jane's life except for this:

> In the year 1784, and at the age of twenty-six Mr. Porter was married. The object of his choice was a lady of decided piety; indeed it would have been unaccountably strange, if, with his religious views he could have united himself to a person of a different description: it would have rendered the very existence of his faith almost dubious, and have been a virtual renunciation of what he had professed on the subject of religion. Soon after his entrance into the married state, he removed to a residence near Guilford [*sic*, Guildford], in Surrey, where he was accustomed to attend the Baptist congregation, of which Mr. J. Chamberlain was the pastor. The preaching of this minister had proved very edifying to Mrs. P., on which account he felt rather attached to his ministry; still it was not altogether satisfactory, on account of Mr. Chamberlain's sentiments on the subject of Baptism. Out of respect however to his wife, who was a Baptist in sentiment, Mr. Porter said but little on the subject.[4]

The following text, probably written by John Paul Porter, presents a woman of deep piety and an ideal pastor's wife. Though little is known about Jane Porter's life, it preserves the dying words of this Baptist woman. Furthermore, Jane Porter's quotations suggest that her spirituality was broadly evangelical,

---

[3] For instance, see Stephen Copson, and Peter Morden, eds., *Challenge and Change: English Baptist Life in the Eighteenth Century* (Didcot: Baptist Historical Society, 2017); J.H.Y. Briggs, and Paul S. Fiddes, eds., *Peoples of God: Baptists and Jews over Four Centuries* (Oxford: Regent's Park College, 2019). Both works have included articles addressing previously ignored topics in Baptist history, such as culture, politics, and gender.

[4] Philip Cater, *Memoirs of the Life and Character of the Late Rev. John Paul Porter, More Than Forty Years Pastor of the First Baptist Church in Buth* (Bath, 1834), 28–29.

as she was well versed in the scriptures and works of Isaac Watts (1674–1748), John Cennick (1718–1755), and Edward Young (1681–1765). As a Baptist, Jane Porter was nourished by evangelical hymns. The text has been carefully transcribed with little changes.

Text[5]

Mrs. Jane Porter, late wife of J.P. Porter, pastor of the Baptist church at Bath, departed this life August 18, 1808; aged 47.[6] She was a native of Guildford in Surrey, and at about the age of 21 was led to attend the ministry of the late Mr. John Chamberlain, pastor of the Baptist congregation in that town, and the Lord was pleased to render his ministry efficacious in turning her from darkness to light.[7] Her convictions were deep, they could not be hid. Many oppositions she experienced in the commencement of her pilgrimage, but the Lord gave her strength according to her day. Embracing the gospel of God her Saviour, she found the Redeemer to be (what every believing soul experiences) "a friend that sticketh closer than a brother" [Prov 18:24]. The holy Spirit enlightened her understanding to see the beauty and glory of Jesus Christ, and to reply wholly on his blood and righteousness for her salvation. She was baptized, with

---

[5] "Mrs. Porter," *Baptist Magazine* 1 (January 1809): 27–28.

[6] John Paul Porter (1759–1832) was born in Richmond, Surrey, and, as an adult, he wished to pursue a legal profession. After experiencing life-threatening thunderstorms, Porter began to attend a dissenting chapel at Kingston in October 1783, where he heard the preaching of John Townsend (d. 1826). Under Townsend, Porter experienced conversion and change. Three months later, Porter joined the Independent church at Kingston. Porter met and married Jane in 1784, and they soon moved to Guildford, Surrey, where they attended the Baptist chapel pastored by John Chamberlain (1723–1792). Through Chamberlain, the Porters were convinced of credobaptism and were baptised as believers. Though Porter declined many ministerial invitation, he moved to Bath in April 1790 and was ordained on August 3, 1791, as the minister of the Baptist congregation on Somerset Street. Under Porter's pastorate, members supporting William Gadsby (1773–1844) were excluded, and Porter was instrumental in the formation of the Old Baptist Chapel at Chippenham in 1804 (J.R. Broome, *John Warburton: Servant of a Covenant God* [Harpenden, Hertfordshire: Gospel Standard Trust, 1996], 141). On Porter's life, see Cater, *Memoirs of the Life and Character of the Late Rev. John Paul Porter*.

[7] John Chamberlain (1723–1792), not to be confused with the missionary John Chamberlain (1777–1821), was the minister at Charcoal Barn Chapel, Guildford, Surrey, from 1757 to 1792. Before coming to Guildford, Chamberlain was at Luton. Though the congregation could be traced back to the seventeenth century, its minute book began in 1744, when Diodat Hoare became its pastor. When Chamberlain died on October 11, 1792, John Rippon (1751–1836) preached his funeral sermon, in which the London minister said, "the soundness of his faith, the simplicity of his manners, the sincerity of his friendship, and the savour of his devotion, rendered him, both in life and death, an ornament to the Christian name, and an honour to the ministerial and pastoral functions" (cited Ralph F. Chambers, *The Strict Baptist Chapels of England Volume I The Chapels of Surrey and Hampshire* [Rushden, Northamptonshire: Strict Baptist Historical Society, 1952], 27). Also see John Rippon, *The Baptist Annual Register, for 1798, 1799, 1800, and Part of 1801* (London, 1801), 34 n.286.

her husband in the summer of 1789, at Wokingham, Berks, by Mr. Thomas Davis of Reading.[8] She was united in fellowship with the Baptist Church at Guildford, and so continued until her removal by providence to Bath, in consequence of her husband's being invited to the pastoral office in that city.

She was the subject of much affliction for eleven years. Her sufferings were very great, and her support was great also. Many Christian friends found it good to visit her, for in her "they saw the grace of God and were glad" [Acts 11:23]. Although confined to her chamber, she was a mother in Israel, and young persons seeking the Lord found her a valuable friend and counsellor. Some friends used to meet every Lord's day evening in her chamber to spend an hour in social prayer. These meetings were profitable to herself and to others, as the recollection of many testifies. But as her weakness increased she was unable to continue them, and they were relinquished.

The Lord brought her by slow degrees to the house appointed for all living. She well knew that death was approaching, and conversed on that subject with the greatest freedom. The fear of death was interely removed, so that she could meet it as a friend to conduct her to glory. Nevertheless she had her infirmities, and felt and lamented them before God. A friend who was standing by her, being deeply affected with her sufferings, took occasion to admire the patience manifested in enduring affliction so sharp and long without complaint; at which she was much displeased, and replied: "Do not say so, I am a poor fretful creature, and my nature is very vile indeed; if it were not so, I should not need so much refining. My heavenly Father would not lay upon me so much affliction if it were not absolutely necessary, for he doth not willingly afflict nor grieve the children of men."

Her latter days were not rapturous, but they were happy; steadily relying upon the atoning blood of Jesus Christ. To a female friend who watched her many nights in the most affectionate manner, she once said, "I have had this night a prelude of heaven for an hour." Her countenance was pleasant, indicating the happy frame of her mind, and many sweet sentences dropped from her lips shewing that she was rich in faith and ripe for glory. She applied the lines of Dr. Watts to herself,

> Now I am dead to all the globe,
> And all the globe is dead to me.[9]

---

[8] Thomas Davis (1734–1796). See Michael A.G. Haykin, *Holy Spirit Now Descend: Thomas Davis and the Evangelical Revival in Georgian Berkshire* (Brighton: Ettrick, 2022).

[9] This quote came from the fourth stanza of Isaac Watts' (1674–1748) famous hymn, "When I survey the wonderous cross." The entire stanza is "His dying Crimson like a Robe/Spreads o'er his Body on the Tree,/Then am I dead to all the Globe,/And all the Globe is dead to me" (Watts, *Hymns and Spiritual Songs* [London, 1707], 189). The original title of this hymn is "Crucifixion to the World by the Cross of Christ;

The last words she was heard to articulate were
The dear Redeemer, dying Lamb,
I love to hear of thee,
No music like thy charming name,
Nor half so sweet can be.[10]

This was about 16 hours before her departure. After this she lay dozing without any signs of pain, and at 12 at noon her soul left the afflicted body, and entered into the joy of her Lord, while her partner in life with the friend above-mentioned were watching her last moments. They then, with the niece of the deceased (whom she had brought up from her infancy and tenderly loved) kneeled down and prayed and blessed the Lord for the grace bestowed upon the deceased, the support granted her, and the deliverance she had just experienced from all pain and sorrow. The feelings of these survivors were wound up to the keenest sensibility. May the awful, pleasing, painful impressions never be effaced.

O the soft commerce! O the tender ties close twisted with the fibres of the heart! Which broken break them, & drain off the soul of human joys, and make it pain to live. And is it thus to live? when such friends part 'Tis the survivor dies.[11]

Mr. Barnard, of Bradford, addressed the congregation at the interment, on the 23rd, and the Lord's day following improved the event to a crowded assembly, from the text she had fixed on for that service, Job xix, 25–27.[12]

Gal. 6.14."

---

[10] The original stanza writes: "Thou dear Redeemer, dying Lamb,/I love to hear of Thee:/No Musick like thy charming Name,/Is half so sweet to me:/O let me ever hear thy Voice,/In Mercy to me speak/And in my Priest will I rejoice, My great Melchisedech" (John Cennick, "Hymn LXXXIV. Thou art a Priest for ever after the Order of Melchisedech," *Sacred Hymns for the Use of Religious Societies* [London, 1764], 3:143). John Cennick (1718–1755) was born in Reading, Berkshire, and experienced conversion at the age of 19. Cennick knew the early leaders of Methodism. On John Wesley's (1703–1791) recommendation, Cennick joined the movement. However, as a Calvinist, Cennick left Wesley's connection and joined himself to George Whitefield (1714–1770). In 1745, he became a Moravian and studied in Germany. As an itinerant preacher, Cennick helped to establish a church in Bath. He died of a fever in London and was buried in Chelsea. Cennick also wrote and published many hymns. On Cennick, see Robert Edmund Cotter, *John Cennick (1718–1755): Methodism, Moravianism and the Rise of Evangelicalism* (Abingdon: Routledge, 2022).

[11] Edward Young, *The Complaint: Or, Night-Thoughts on Life, Death, and Immortality* (London, 1745), 2:43.

[12] James Barnard ministered at the Old Baptist Chapel at Bradford-on-Avon, Wiltshire. See Robert W. Oliver, *Baptists in Bradford on Avon. The History of the Old Baptist Church Bradford on Avon 1689–1989* (Bradford on Avon: Old Baptist Chapel, 1989).

"Dr. M will go down": Joseph Kinghorn (1766–1832) on two Baptist controversies

ed. Baiyu Andrew Song

Baiyu Andrew Song FRAS is the assistant professor of general education studies at Heritage College and Seminary, Cambridge, ON, and an adjunct lecturer at Redeemer University, Ancaster, ON.

Introduction

When John Stoughton (1807–1897) wrote about the English Baptist life in the first decades of the nineteenth century, the Norwich-born Congregationalist historian pointed out how "the hypercalvinistic controversy, the communion controversy, and the Serampore controversy" had impacted members of the Baptist world.[1] Though these controversies seem to be unrelated, scholars like W.R. Ward have suggested that Fullerism was a primary factor that "greatly increased the pressure for open communion amongst the Baptists," which he explained as a result of having "theological modernism and popular appeal … go hand in hand."[2] Though English Particular Baptists had debated the terms of communion since the seventeenth century, the communion controversy featuring Robert Hall, Jr. (1764–1831) and Joseph Kinghorn (1766–1832) took place at a turning point of the denomination and the English society. By and large, all three controversies concerned the denomination's identity. The latter two should be understood especially in the context of the increasing pressure

---

[1] John Stoughton, *History of Religion in England from the Opening of the Long Parliament to 1850. Volume VII Church of the First Half of the 19th Century*, 2nd ed. (London: Hodder and Stoughton, 1901), 262.

[2] W.R. Ward, *Religion and Society in England 1790–1850* (London: B.T. Batsford, 1972), 19.

of denominational institutionalisation and evangelical catholicity. In other words, while Fullerism opened the door for Particular Baptists to once again actively engage in evangelistic activities, the spirit of unity and cooperation inspired them to look beyond their "walled gardens" to fulfil their passion for the gospel's spread in both the British Isles and the world.[3]

Unlike popular depictions, the communion controversy in the early nineteenth century took off first among the missionaries in correspondence between Serampore and Kettering, as newly-arrived missionaries like William Ward (1769–1823) and Joshua Marshman (1768–1837) practiced open communion and persuaded the mission station to adopt such a position in 1805. In a series of correspondence (1800–1811) between Ward and Andrew Fuller (1754–1815), the secretary patiently explained why the new position was doctrinally and practically problematic. Though Fuller failed to persuade Ward, his letters helped Marshman to overturn his position, and subsequently, the mission station returned to close communion. In his letter to Fuller on August 31, 1811, Marshman reported that "the Church of Christ at Serampore has restored its primitive and scriptural purity [sic] in point of communion, and I think is not very likely soon to lose it again."[4] Nevertheless, Marshman told Fuller that Ward "candidly opposed it, yet w[ould] not break the peace of the church."[5] Though the issue was fixed on the mission field, this private exchange of opinions marked the tension between the two camps. With his vision for a united and catholic Baptist denomination, and disagreement with Robert Robinson's (1735–1790) brief response to Abraham Booth (1734–1806), Hall published *On Terms of Communion* around July 1, 1815.[6] Hall thus initiated

---

[3] Raymond Brown noticed that "the evangelical revival brought many Particular Baptists into direct contact with a form of Calvinistic theology which insisted on the importance not only of preaching to the unconverted ... but also of offering Christ's mercy with uninhibited compassion" (Brown, *The English Baptists of the Eighteenth Century* [London: Baptist Historical Society, 1986], 91).

[4] Joshua Marshman, Letter to Andrew Fuller, August 31, 1811, as quoted by E. Daniel Potts, "'I Throw Away the Guns to Preserve the Ship': A Note on the Serampore Trio," *Baptist Quarterly* 20.3 (1963): 117.

[5] Andrew Fuller, Letter to William Ward, October 7, 1811, D/FUL, Andrew Fuller Letters (Angus Library and Archive, Regent's Park College, Oxford), 5.

[6] Robert Robinson, *The General Doctrine of Toleration Applied to the Particular Case of Free Communion* (Cambridge, 1781); Abraham Booth, *An Apology for the Baptists* (London, 1778).

Robert Hall, Jr., *On Terms of Communion; With a Particular View to the Case of the Baptists and Pædobaptists* (Leicester, 1815). A number of scholars have mistaken the date of its first publication. For instance, Angus Hamilton MacLeod believed that Hall published his *On Terms of Communion* in the autumn of 1815 ("The Life and Teaching of Robert Hall, 1764–1831" [M.Litt. dissertation, Durham University, 1958], 290). Others, such as Peter Naylor, mistakenly used its first American edition and argued that Hall entered the controversy in 1816 (*Calvinism, Communion and the Baptists: A Study of English Calvinistic Baptists from the Late 1600s to the Early 1800s* [Carlisle, Cumbria; Waynesboro, GA: Paternoster, 2003], 128). It is significant to recognise the date of the publication of the first edition of Hall's *On Terms of Communion*, as it helps us to

another round of pamphlet debates over the terms of communion. In all, more than twenty-one pamphlets were published on both sides. Judging from the tone of some of these pamphlets, the debate was a deeply emotional one, as both sides indulged in *ad hominem* arguments and attacks. Some even called the close communionists "bigots," for instance.[7]

In the following text, Kinghorn mentioned the publication of his *Arguments against the Practice of Mixed Communion*, which was a response to Hall's *A Short Statement of the Reasons for Christian, in Opposition to Party Communion*, published on October 7, 1826.[8] Though Kinghorn had previously responded to Hall in 1816 and 1820, this short work was published as a summary of the controversy.[9] In this work, Kinghorn reaffirmed his argument that since baptism as a divine institution was instituted before the Lord's Supper, credobaptism was prerequisite to Christian communion. Furthermore, Kinghorn warned that Hall's proposal would eliminate denominational identity, as open communion abandoned baptism as an initiatory sacrament. In his letter to Simon Wilkin (1790–1862), Kinghorn's former ward and close friend, the Norwich minister explained his observations and fears. Kinghorn's observation accurately described the changes and challenges the Particular Baptists and even

---

understand why William Newman published Andrew Fuller's manuscript on the same subject, though it was against the latter's initial desires. In Hall's letter to John Ryland, Jr., dated June 17, 1815, the Leicester pastor told his friend after discussing the potential successor of the late Andrew Fuller at the BMS that "My mixed communion will I trust be in about a fortnight" (Robert Hall, Jr., Letter to John Ryland, Jr., June 17, 1815, DA20/1/1, Papers of R. Hall [Special Collections, University of Birmingham, Birmingham], 3). Geoffrey F. Nuttall notes that "my mixed communion" is Hall's *On Terms of Communion* ("Letters from Robert Hall to John Ryland 1791–1824," *Baptist Quarterly* 34.3 [1991]: 129). Thus, Hall's *On Terms of Communion* was probably printed and made available in the market around July 1, 1815.

[7] For instance, in Andrew Gunton Fuller's (1799–1884) memoir of his father, commenting on Andrew Fuller's posthumous tract on close communion, the son wrote: "This publication, though not without marks of that shrewd and penetrating judgment which distinguished his controversial writings, is not remarkable for the most conclusive reasoning; and though it were too much to admit the justice of Mr. [Robert] Hall's insinuation, that his mind was not fully made up on the subject, there is perhaps reason to suppose that a more ample discussion would have effected a considerable alteration in his views. The charge of bigotry, however, made against him, and others cherishing the same sentiments on this subject, says little for the understanding or charity of those who prefer it. True charity will never require the surrender of a man's principles as an evidence of his candour; and happy they who have learned that an honest refusal to unite in the partial use of some minor tokens of affection may consist with the exercise of the tenderest feelings of Christian love" (Andrew Gunton Fuller, *Memoir* in *The Complete Works of the Rev. Andrew Fuller*, ed. Joseph Belcher [Reprint, Harrisonburg, VA: Sprinkle, 1988], 1:100).

[8] Joseph Kinghorn, *Arguments against the Practice of Mixed Communion, and in Support of Communion on the Plan of the Apostolic Church; with Preliminary Observations on Rev. R. Hall's Reasons for Christian, in Opposition to Party Communion* (London; Norwich, 1827).

[9] Joseph Kinghorn, *Baptism a Term of Communion at the Lord's Table* (Norwich, 1816); idem, *A Defence of "Baptism a Term of Communion." In Answer to the Rev. Robert Hall's Reply* (Norwich, 1820).

English dissenters faced towards the end of the Georgian era.[10]

In the second part of his letter, Kinghorn mentioned that being a member of the central committee, he was scheduled to attend the annual meeting of the Baptist Missionary Society, hosted by the Devonshire Square congregation from June 19 to 21, 1827.[11] The purpose of the meeting was to solve the strained relationship between Serampore and the BMS home committee. The Serampore controversy roughly dated from Fuller's death in 1815 to the death of Marshman in 1837. As Brian Stanley understood it, "the roots of the controversy were embedded in the status of the Serampore mission as a largely self-supporting entity—a status which was founded on fundamental principle, and not merely on economic necessity."[12] For William Carey (1761–1834), Ward, and Marshman, the BMS committee was primarily a recruiting and fundraising agency.[13] By becoming financially independent, the Serampore missionaries had little domestic control. Thus, for Carey, "the nub of the issue was not the Serampore property, but the Society's claim to dominion over the membership and funds of the private family, work, and personal finances."[14] As the BMS became institutionalised, the home committee began to see the missionaries as servants and employees. Thus, the missionary society was "a body of expatriate workers,

---

[10] Also see J.H.Y. Briggs, *The English Baptists of the Nineteenth Century* (Didcot, Oxfordshire: Baptist Historical Society, 1994); Michael John Walker, *Baptists at the Table: The Theology of the Lord's Supper amongst English Baptists in the Nineteenth Century* (Didcot, Oxfordshire: Baptist Historical Society, 1992).

[11] "Missionary Herald: Annual Meeting of the Baptist Missionary Society," *Baptist Magazine* 19 (July 1827): 338. Notice the difference between the general committee and the central committee. The general committee of 1827 had 42 ministerial members and 12 messengers. The central committee had 17 ministerial members and 8 messengers. These seventeen ministerial members were: Caleb Evans Birt (1795–1854) of Portsea; John Chin (1773–1839) of Walworth; William Copley of Oxford (married Esther Hewlett Copley in 1827, and later became an alcoholic while ministering in Eythorne, Kent. He later left his wife and ministry in 1843. See Marion Ann Taylor, and Heather E. Weir, eds., *Let Her Speak for Herself: Nineteenth-Century Women Writing on the Women of Genesis* [Waco, TX: Baylor University Press, 2006], 32); F.A. Cox (1783–1853) of Hackney; Richard Davis (1768–1832) of Walworth; Thomas C. Edmonds (1784–1860) of Cambridge; William Giles (1771–1845) of Chatham; William Gray (1776–1848) of Northampton; William Groser (1791–1856) of Maidstone; John Howard Hinton (1791–1873) of Reading; Joseph Ivimey (1773–1834) of London; Joseph Kinghorn of Norwich; Isaac Mann (1785–1831) of London; C.T. Mileham (d. 1829) of Bow; William Newman (1773–1835) of Bow; George Pritchard (1773–1852) of London; James Upton (1759–1834) of London ("Missionary Herald. Baptist Mission. Annual Meeting," *Baptist Magazine* 19 [August 1827]: 393–394).

[12] Brian Stanley, *The History of the Baptist Missionary Society 1792–1992* (Edinburgh: T&T Clark, 1992), 57.

[13] Stanley, *History of the Baptist Missionary Society*, 66. Also see Joseph Ivimey, *Letters on the Serampore Controversy, Addressed to the Rev. Christopher Anderson; Occasioned by a Postscript, Dated Edinburgh, 26th November, 1830, Affixed to the "Reply" of the Rev. D. Marshman* (London, 1831), 128.

[14] Stanley, *History of the Baptist Missionary Society*, 66.

who were responsible to the home Committee that sent them to the field, and ultimately to the subscribers who provided the funds."[15] Such an attitude was clearly revealed in the report. In 1826, Marshman returned to England and sought to reconcile with the committee, and secure a royal charter for the Serampore College from Frederick VI of Denmark (1768–1839). For the BMS committee, "it was felt objectionable, indeed, that the stations had been, and all their contemplated missionary efforts were to remain, identified with the college."[16]

The college was founded independently of the Serampore missionaries in 1818, but it had faced financial challenges since its foundation.[17] Furthermore, even within the Serampore mission, criticism was raised for "the breadth of its curriculum and its readiness to admit non-Christian students."[18] With its increasing financial needs, the Serampore mission applied to the BMS committee for financial support. At their meetings, Marshman rejected both John Dyer's (1783–1841) and Joseph Gutteridge's (1752–1844) proposals, as he insisted that the council of the Serampore College should be the only managing body of the Serampore stations.[19] The BMS committee thus refused to sponsor the college, which "owed no corporate responsibility to the BMS."[20] On March 23, 1827, the BMS committee publicly announced the separation of the Serampore Mission.

It is curious to consider Kinghorn's comments on the controversy and Marshman in his letter to Wilkin. Nevertheless, it should be read in light of his public speech at the annual meeting. The *Baptist Magazine* recorded the following speech by Joseph Kinghorn at the annual meeting in June 1827:

---

[15] Stanley, *History of the Baptist Missionary Society*, 66.

[16] "Missionary Herald: Annual Meeting of the Baptist Missionary Society," 339.

[17] On the foundation of the college, see D.A. Christadoss, "The Story of Serampore College, 1818–1929" in *The Story of Serampore and Its College*, ed. Wilma S. Stewart (Serampore: Council of Serampore College, 1961), 20–27. Interestingly, just a few months later, the Ultra-Ganges Mission of the London Missionary Society (LMS) founded the Anglo-Chinese College on November 11, 1818, in Malacca by Robert Morrison (1782–1834) and William Milne (1785–1822). It could not be coincidence, as there was a friendly competition between the two mission stations for translating and printing the first Chinese Bible. The Anglo-Chinese College received support from the LMS. See William Milne, *A Retrospect of the First Ten Years of the Protestant Mission to China* (Malacca: Anglo-Chinese Press, 1820); Robert Morrison, *To the Public, Concerning the Anglo-Chinese College* (Malacca: Mission Press, 1823); Brian Harrison, *Waiting for China: The Anglo-Chinese College at Malacca, 1818–1843, and Early Nineteenth-Century Missions* (Hong Kong: Hong Kong University Press, 1979); R.L. O'Sullivan, "The Anglo-Chinese College and the Early 'Singapore Institution,'" *Journal of the Malaysian Branch of the Royal Asiatic Society* 61.2 (1988): 45–62.

[18] Stanley, *History of the Baptist Missionary Society*, 63–64.

[19] See Stanley, *History of the Baptist Missionary Society*, 64–65.

[20] Stanley, *History of the Baptist Missionary Society*, 65.

The Rev. Joseph Kinghorn said that the committee had been looking forward to this day with concern and anxiety. Having passed through a crisis, involving more than common responsibility, they have been particularly anxious that their fidelity to the trust reposed in them should be evidenced to the Society. They have taken all possible means to preserve the union, but in vain. The correspondence and discussion were long and tedious. You will remember the impossibility of quick communications with persons in so distant a land. We have had to exercise patience. We have made various efforts and offered many prayers that those efforts might be successful. We have done all we could to prevent such a report as this being read to you today. You also have been looking forward to this day with anxiety. The movements of the committee plainly indicated that something very particular was under consideration; and in our several connexions and neighbourhoods we have often been asked what was going forward—and we have been obliged to give some answers to these inquiries. Now the matter has been brought to a conclusion, we present an account of our proceedings, which we trust will obtain your approbation and sanction. We regret the separation, but we were driven to the measure. Yet, though cast down, we are not destroyed. We have only been in this situation in which many better men have been before us. There has never been a good cause without any difficulties. All voyages are liable to storms. Christianity itself has had its difficulties. Though we have been exercised with a storm, we are not cast down. Do not you be cast down; do not, by frowning upon us, diminish our energies or our hopes. Those who drew up the Report which has been read, have acted wisely in stating fully and fairly what has been done. We found ourselves compelled by a sense of duty to resist the demands that were made. We were entrusted with the gifts of your liberality, the object of which has been constantly expressed in your annual reports to be for preaching the Gospel to the heathen. The sums that have been given, to the brethren at Serampore, were only to assist in the support of their Missionary stations; and we required accounts of the manner in which these monies should be dispensed, and of the progress made in the work of the Lord at the respective stations. Such accounts we required, not from any suspicion of our brethren at Serampore, but to enable us to answer any inquiries that might be made of us at home. We were never consulted upon the building of the College, and we have not felt ourselves called upon to give any opinion on the propriety or impropriety of the undertaking. We leave this to those who have built it. We do not deny that many advantages may be derived by the natives of India from the cultivation of literature. Whether much good has ever been done by colleges and universities, in extending the kingdom of Christ, that kingdom which is not of this world, may perhaps be questioned; but however this may have been, the establishment of a college formed not part of your plan, and we could not, without manifest injustice to you, appropriate any part of your funds to this purpose. We have no objection to literature, to the extension of literature, or to the means of doing it. It is an instrument of great usefulness, when properly directed, of which the world knows not the value. Many a man has been deemed an idler when labouring hard in literary studies; but it has afterwards been evident that he was preparing for the future service of the church. But we are your stewards, and stewards should be faithful to the trust reposed in them. Our appeal is you. If you think, that on the whole we have acted faithfully in regarding your interests and dispensing your liberality, you will signify your approbation, and sanction what we have done. But whatever you may think of the conduct of your committee, or whether you may be pleased to elect one of us again, we trust you will go on with your exertions in the cause. But we must entreat you to help us by your prayers. Think of the important consequences dependent on the deliberations of a few obscure men composing your committee. An oppressive feeling of this often rests upon our minds: we are legislating for millions; the immortal interests of millions of our fellow-men, are involved in our decisions; according as things appear to us, we send missionaries to one station or to another. We need the best influences to direct us. Pray that we may be guided aright. We beseech you to be united among yourselves as you have hitherto been. And whenever you pray for yourselves pray also for this Society, and for all missionary Societies, and for the success of missions in every part of the world.[21]

Kinghorn's consistency reflected the deeply rooted differences between the home committee and the Serampore missionaries. Furthermore, the Serampore controversy, though unfortunate, illustrated the changing culture within the Particular Baptist community in England.

Text[22]
Norwich June 4. 1827
My dear S.——

---

[21] "Missionary Herald: Annual Meeting of the Baptist Missionary Society," *Baptist Magazine* 19 (July 1827): 345–346.

[22] Joseph Kinghorn, Letter to Simon Wilkin, June 4, 1827, #108, "Wilkin papers," MC64/12, 508X8 (Norfolk Record Office, Norwich).

I have rec^d. both your letters,^23 and will write a line——tho' I have nothing to say——I wish you were home again——and better than before. I want to have Slee printed——If you do not make haste, take care lest there is not another tract clamouring for publicity!——The piece on Communion is out,^24 & going about—some do not like it——others do——I am satisfied, that whatever may be said of the execution——the design was right—— I believe the tendency is, & will be right; for under a change of circumstances in a few things, our church would be thrown into unspeakable confusion, if the inclinations of some are not counteracted——But the most high rules——Churches as well as individuals want trials, and I often think, it is the case with us——at how low an ebb, is serious, earnest, feeling, religion! It gives me many an alarm. I often say to myself, things cannot go on thus! But, alas, it is not me alone, our Denomination at large, is not in good state; nor does the evil end here, I strongly suspect that other denominations——are as bad or worse, and one general tendency is working through the whole; a cold indifferent laxity——in doctrine and in practice. The general profession of the present day will do very little against this downhill tendency, it will add materials to the mass, rolling on in that direction; and the few cases in which strong impressions may lead some to expostulate will only call forth the clamour of others against them. It is an unspeakable mercy where grace forms the character, with an energy that makes it abound in the work of the Lord——

While in Lond°.. enquire into the price &c of Assemani Bibliothica Orientalis^25 4 vol. [Fo.?]. It would be a heavy purchase I fear, for an individual ~~but~~ & disliked by our L.L. Text. but it is a pity, there should not be one in Norwich somewhere. At least ask questions about it.

If all is well, I shall endeavour to be in Lond°.. at the Annual meetg——Some things in the affair I do not like——it will on many acco^ts be an anxious time, but I have had so much concern in the business of the past year, that it would be like fearfulness or cowardice not to be there without some prominent reason, otherwise, I should ~~have~~ rather not ~~have give~~ have the trouble of it just

---

[23] These refer to two letters that Simon Wilkin wrote to Kinghorn in May 1827. On May 7, 1827, Wilkin and his wife Emma (née Culley) left Norwich and arrived in London on May 18, after spending some time in Cambridge. The first letter was undated and the second letter was written on May 29. See Simon Wilkin, Letter to Joseph Kinghorn, undated, #106, "Wilkin papers," MC64/12, 508X8 (Norfolk Record Office, Norwich); Simon Wilkin, Letter to Joseph Kinghorn, May 29, 1827, #107, "Wilkin papers," MC64/12, 508X8 (Norfolk Record Office, Norwich). In these letters, Wilkin mentioned he heard sermons by two Scottish ministers, Thomas Chalmers (1780–1847) and Robert Gordon (1786–1853).

[24] Kinghorn, *Arguments against the Practice of Mixed Communion*.

[25] Giuseppe Simone Assemani (1687–1768), *Bibliotheca Orientalis Clementino-Vaticana* (Rome: Typis Sacræ Congregationis de Propaganda Fide, 1719).

now——I have had a letter from Mr. Dyer who says a little about the state of things,[26] from which——and from my former knowledge——& impression, I think D^r. M will go down——and must go down;[27]——not without doing mischief——but he ~~will~~ himself will <u>go down</u>, and if fame & family aggrandisement be his object, or if through the deep delusion of the human heart, his easily besetting sin is hidden from his own view, still, <u>he</u> & <u>his</u>, <u>will</u>, and <u>must</u> be so far pushed into notice, that the development of what has passed and is passing, will suck their Credit. The committee might do wrong in the case you refer to; I know their defence, in part at least, and there is something in it, I own I never was thoroughly satisfied, so as to be <u>convinced</u> that they were right, but if error it was, it was on the right side, and eventually will hurt D^r. M. more than the Committee. Pride drives a brisk trade, but it is always, a losing concern. The history of the Kingdom of God, is not the history of splendid Colleges. Humility is the way to utility & honour. "When ~~Israel~~ Ephraim spake trembling he exalted himself in Israel." (Hos. 13.1.) But here comes a reason for giving over; the paper is full. Love to Mrs.——Yours, affect^y.

                                                                            J. Kinghorn.

---

[26] John Dyer (1783–1841), served as the first full-time secretary of the Baptist Missionary Society since 1818. Dyer's letter is not in any Kinghorn collections.

[27] Here Kinghorn refers to Joshua Marshman (1768–1837), who received an honourary Doctor of Divinity degree from Brown University, Providence, RI, in 1811. Marshman visited England from June 1826 to February 1829.

Book reviews

Jason Matossian, *James Owen and the Defense of Moderate Nonconformity*, Reformed Historical Theology 71 (Göttingen: Vandenhoeck & Ruprecht, 2022), 166 pages.

In the heat of the debate between the Establishment and nonconformity in the seventeenth and eighteenth centuries, one may think that there were only two clerical options: either conform to the Church of England or become a strict separatist. However, there was a more moderate position held by those who wanted to minister in nonconformist churches and yet hold to certain degrees of conformity with the Church of England. Such a position is known as moderate nonconformity, the view held and argued for by James Owen (1654–1706). In this monograph, Matossian helpfully shows the historical context for the moderate nonconformist position, as well as the place that James Owen, a Welsh Presbyterian, had within it.

The first two chapters open the work by offering the historical background for the debate over nonconformity. Matossian surveys the relevant literature to present the place of the moderate nonconformist position, and places emphasis on Richard Baxter (1615–1691) as an important figure in this movement. The third chapter focuses more specifically on the values of the moderate nonconformists, which involved four key ideas: "charity," "unity in doctrine," "separation without schism," and "Lordship of Christ over conscience." Chapter four then looks at Owen's sources of authority, which Matossian argues were Scripture, the providence of God, and the history of the church. A survey of the controversy between Owen and Thomas Gipps (d. 1709) forms the heart of chapter five. Whereas the former argued for the legitimacy of ordinations outside the Church of England, the latter, as an ordained Anglican, argued against it. The sixth chapter is on the issue of "occasional conformity, wherein those whose commitment was to a Nonconformist church participated in Anglican worship and communion on occasion" (p.121). The chapter first presents Owen's argument before then looking at the variety of responses that he received. The book closes with a conclusion followed by a bibliography and two indexes—one of subjects, the other of persons.

Overall, this work is a welcome addition to the very slim amount of scholarship on James Owen and moderate nonconformity and some of the responses to it. Owen is not a well-known figure, and to have a study dedicated to his intellectual engagements is an important contribution to the scholarship of this era. But, in addition to being a welcome study from a historical perspective, it is also a timely book for pastors and other Christian leaders in our current context. As catholicity is a popular and important topic in contemporary studies, Matossian has nicely shown how one group of Christians desired unity despite differences.

Jonathan N. Cleland
PhD cand., Knox College, University of Toronto
Toronto, Ontario, Canada

Michael A.G. Haykin, *The Missionary Fellowship of William Carey* (Sanford, FL: Reformation Trust Publishing, 2018), 161 pages.

William Carey (1761–1834) not only stands a legend in Baptist history, but this cobbler-turned-missionary continues to be one of the most admired figures in church history overall. Unsurprisingly, a celebrity culture began to develop around him toward the end of his life. In response, Carey told his nephew Eustace Carey: "I am a plodder, it is true. I have no genius, but I can plod" (p.3). Yet while Carey's name is known, the friends who contributed to his theological development are often overlooked. In this work Michael Haykin remedies this gap, detailing the impact of the various men who influenced Carey to become the pioneer missionary that he was.

By way of introduction, Haykin, cites Christopher Anderson (1782–1852), a Scottish Baptist leader who knew several of the men in Carey's life (which included Andrew Fuller [1754–1815], John Ryland Jr. [1753–1825], John Sutcliff [1752–1814], and Samuel Pearce [1766–1799]). Anderson described them as a "little band of brothers" who spread Christianity throughout the world (p.7). At this point Haykin makes his secondary intention clear, by offering a word on the modern depletion of such fraternity. As friendship continues to be on a decline in modern society, he notes, "True friendships take time and sacrifice, and Western culture in the early twenty-first century is a busy world that as a rule is far more interested in receiving and possessing than sacrificing and giving" (p.10). The impact of friendship in Carey's life, therefore, shows the ability of iron to sharpen iron.

Haykin first traces how friendship shaped Carey from the early stages of his life. For instance, as a young man Carey became friends with his fellow apprentice-shoemaker, John Warr who himself was a Congregationalist. Having been raised Anglican, Carey initially resisted Warr's pressure to reconsider his religious commitment, but eventually accompanied Warr to a Dissenters' midweek prayer service in Hackleton. This relationship proved pivotal. It led Carey initially to try to reform his life, only to later realize the mercy he needed was to "depend on a crucified Saviour for pardon and salvation, and to seek a system of doctrines in the word of God" (p.19). Carey's life was altered completely—joining himself with the Congregationalists, marrying his first wife Dorothy (1756–1807), and even occasionally preaching at Hackleton and at Earls Barton to a group of Baptists. It was here where he met Sutcliff and Fuller.

Carey's introduction to Particular Baptist life through these men at the Northamptonshire Baptist Association caused him to question pedobaptism. He definitively joined their ranks on October 5, 1786, through the guidance of John Ryland Sr. (1723–1792) and his son, John Ryland Jr. He subsequently became a member Sutcliff's church in Olney, and only thirteen months later was ordained to pastor a church in Moulton. Ryland Jr., Fuller, and Sutcliff all participated in his ordination. Within this evangelical-Calvinistic context, Carey developed a passion for the gospel to be taken to the ends of the earth. At one point his enthusiasm apparently earned a rebuke from the elder Ryland in a pastor's gathering. While there is dispute regarding the precise nature of this rebuke, Haykin explains that "[t]he preponderance of evidence, however, does seem to indicate that Carey did receive some sort of stinging rebuke from the elder Ryland" (p.40). Haykin resists the insistence by some that Carey had to be an Arminian due to his passion for evangelism and missions, asserting, "To put it plainly: without understanding Carey's consistent delight in Calvinism throughout his life, we cannot understand the man, his motivation, or eventually the shape of his mission" (p.4).

It was not only his conversion and journey to Baptist convictions that stemmed from friendship, however. Haykin notes that the mission to India itself developed out of these relationships, which played out in the context of associational life in Northamptonshire. This group of friends around Carey sought to persuade the churches of the necessity to carry the gospel to the world. Sutcliff's "Prayer Call" (1784), which was based on the ministry of Jonathan Edwards (1703–1758), was a vital step towards the formation of the Baptist Missionary Society. In his treatise *An Enquiry into the Obligations of Christians, to Use Means for the Conversion of the Heathens* (1792), Carey answered objections raised by hyper-Calvinists, provided a mini-history of missions, gave a statistical table of the countries of the world with their population numbers and religious persuasion, and addressed pragmatic objections. Carey also preached the associational message that came to be known as the "Deathless Sermon," in which he exhorted the churches to "expect great things" and "attempt great things" in missions—which resulted in the formation of a committee to consider establishing a "Baptist society for propagating the gospel among the heathens" (p.80). On October 2, 1792, at Kettering, fourteen men squeezed into the parlor of Martha Wallis (a member of Fuller's church) to explore this idea. One person described the attendees as being "of no fame and of scantiest salary" and who were "nobodies from nowhere" (p.83). Out of this gathering though, the world changed, for the society would appoint Carey along with John Thomas (1757–1801) as the first two missionaries.

Haykin also unpacks the significance of Carey's missionary friendships. To begin with, Carey's wife had been reluctant to go to India before John Thomas persuaded her to accompany her husband. While in India, Dorothy descended into mental instability after the death of their third son Peter (1789–94), from which she never recovered. Following her death in 1807, Carey married Charlotte Rumohr (1761–1821), who battled her own illness until her death in 1821. Carey later married his last wife Grace Hughes (1778–1835), who cared for Carey in his final days. Alongside these deaths, there were other challenges in India, which were eased by the arrival of two co-laborers: Joshua Marshman (1768–1837) and William Ward (1769–1823). Known as the Serampore Trio, these men's personalities and talents complemented one another in the work of Bible translation, education, and evangelism. Haykin highlights Carey's description of the friendship between them accordingly: "As the image or shadow bigotry is not known among us here, we take sweet counsel together, and go to the house of God as friends" (p.99).

Sadly, when the initial advocates for missionary work—Fuller, Sutcliff, and Ryland Jr.—died, alienation and separation marked the relationship of the Serampore mission and the London headquarters of the Baptist Missionary Society. Yet Carey's commitment to Christ did not waver. Haykin points to a letter written by Carey to son Jabez near the end of his life, saying, "I trust for acceptance with him to the blood of Christ alone; and I hope I am received into the divine favor through him" (p.118). This commitment to Christ and this deeper love for him was rooted in the friendships God provided him.

It is for these reasons that Haykin's work on William Carey, while not an exhaustive biography, is a superb resource to better understand the development of Carey by the means of godly friendships—whether in the years immediately following his conversion and early theological development, or as the advocate of missions in England, or in staying faithful amidst difficulties in India.

The necessity for modern churches to cultivate friendships becomes self-evident through this account. To this end, Haykin also provides two resources in the appendices to show the theological commitments of Carey. The first, "The Leicester Covenant," Carey wrote at his second pastorate in England at Harvey Lane Baptist Church, in order to lead the church in reconstituting itself. The second, "The Serampore Agreement," governed the Baptist mission in Serampore. It well displays the theological commitments of the Trio and how various Christian truths were to be lived out in the church and society. If someone is looking to be stirred by the power of Christian friendship, this book is a must-read.

Jake Stone, MDiv student
The Southern Baptist Theological Seminary
Louisville, Kentucky

William Carey, *An Enquiry: A Modern Edition of a Missions Classic*, ed. Lea Eppling; Foreword by Paige Patterson, Afterword by David Eppling (1792, Cleveland, GA: TMU Press, 2021), 83 pages.

This fresh edition of the famous book by William Carey (1761–1834), rightly described as a "Missions Classic" in the sub-title, is indeed welcome. The original edition of his *An Enquiry into the Obligations of Christians, to Use Means for the Conversion of the Heathens* was published in 1792 by a Leicester bookseller, Ann Ireland. It was reprinted in 1818 (the title page of this edition is reprinted on page 9) and in 1892 (the centennial of the original publication). It was republished as a whole again in 1934 (the centenary of Carey's death), 1961, (the bicentennial of the author's birth), and then again in 1988. Carey was not a theologian and, apart from this remarkable text, he left very little by way of theological tracts or treatises. Hence the importance of this text. The spelling and grammar of this edition have been lightly modernized so as to enable Carey's eighteenth-century prose to speak as powerfully to a modern audience as it did to men and women of his day. One major section, Carey's tabulation of the nations of his day in terms of their size, population, and religion, has been moved to the close of the book as an addendum.

Carey's text lays out the missional implications of Matthew 28:19–20 (p.15–17) and answers objections to the missionary endeavour (p.18–20 and 47–54). He rehearses the history of the church's involvement in mission, in both the Scriptures and across the centuries since the Apostolic era (p.21–39). He obviously believes that past patterns of mission and evangelism have been recorded for both inspiration and imitation. He is especially impressed with the missions undertaken by the Moravians. "None of the moderns have equaled" their missionary undertakings, he comments (p.38–39). The final section of the treatise deals with the practicalities of mission: the vital necessity of prayer—"the most glorious works of grace that have ever taken place have been in answer to prayer (p.56); and the necessity of forming a missions society that can select missionaries and raise finances for them (p.58–62).

Paige Patterson's introduction to this new edition of puts Carey's tract into the context of his life in England and mission in India (p.5–7). He stresses that one key impact of this tract was that it "constituted the weapon used by God to explode the Calvinistic closed mind to human obligation to take the gospel to the earth's end" (p.7). Of course, Carey, as Dr. Patterson knows, remained a Particular, that is, Calvinistic, Baptist all of his life. In its emphasis on human obligation, highlighted in the tract's title, Carey's *Enquiry* was a re-affirmation of a biblical Calvinism that emphasized equally divine sovereignty and human responsibility. It was indeed a weapon in the hands of a holy God: not against the mindset of Calvinism per se, but against what is properly denoted as hyper-Calvinism, or what Carey's close friend Andrew Fuller (noted on p.7) called "False Calvinism." This was a theological perspective that so emphasized divine sovereignty that it was closed to the free offer of the Gospel and thus had neither passion nor interest in mission.

In the concluding paragraph of his "Foreword," Dr. Patterson extends his thanks to Drs Emir Caner, the president of Truett McConnell University, and Peter Lumpkins, the associate professor of history and missions at the University, for recognizing the importance of publishing this new edition of Carey's *Enquiry*. I join my thanks to his and hope that many more readers will be equally thankful.

Michael A.G. Haykin
The Southern Baptist Theological Seminary

Andrew Roberts, *The Last King of America: The Misunderstood Reign of George III* (New York, NY: Viking, 2021), 784 pages.

The best biographers give their readers a window not only into the life of their subject, but also into the world in which their subject lived. Andrew Roberts' recent work on King George III (1738–1820) is a model example of this kind of work. It provides not only an unprecedented look into a major historical figure, but also a sweeping overview of the socio-political setting of the eighteenth-century trans-Atlantic period. Over the last decade or so, Roberts has established himself as a leading biographer of major historical subjects, with award-winning publications such as *Napoleon: A Life* (2014) and *Churchill: Walking with Destiny* (2018). Major periodicals such as *The Wall Street Journal* and *The Washington Post* have praised Roberts not only for the depth of his historical scholarship, but also for the engaging nature of his writing. In *The Last King of America: The Misunderstood Reign of George III*, Roberts has once again sought to tackle a prominent historical figure, by focusing on the life and reign of one of Britain's most polarizing monarchs.

Roberts is not the first historian to try and engage the complexities of King George. His work, however, is groundbreaking because it is the first major biography of this King to incorporate more than 200,000 pages of Hanoverian documents that were previously sealed in the royal archives until 2015. With unprecedented access to this wealth of primary source material, Roberts hopes to introduce readers to "the true story of George III" (p.4).

Roberts' project in *The Last King of America* is undoubtedly an ambitious one. He frames his study of George III around the idea that the eighteenth-century monarch is "the most unfairly traduced sovereign in the long history of British monarchy" (p.4). For a prime example of how this subject has been falsely represented in the centuries after his lifetime, Roberts uses the portrayal of George III as a "comic, yet cruel" tyrant in the Broadway hit *Hamilton: An American Musical* (p.1). Roberts blames this misunderstanding on the prevailing narratives of some of George's eighteenth-century contemporaries, such as Thomas Paine (1737–1809) and Thomas Jefferson (1743–1826), as well as subsequent generations of British Whig and Liberal historians who despised the King (p.2). As an antidote to these alleged historical misrepresentations, Roberts declares that his intention is to let George III speak on his own terms—that way it is on the basis of facts that modern readers may make their judgement (p.4).

In his survey, Roberts is not shy about making decisive positive assessments of the King's character and religious faith. He describes George as the "only uxorious husband and pious Christian" of the Hanoverian dynasty, which was plagued by sexual infidelity (p.48); a "civilized, good-natured, Christian and enlightened monarch" (p.308–309); "personally virtuous … a pious Christian, honest, humane … immensely stoical in the face of a truly horrific recurring illness" (p.657); and "well-meaning, hard-working, decent, dutiful, moral, cultured, and kind" (p.676). Roberts does not shirk, however, from highlighting the King's political and moral blunders. For instance, he points to George's seemingly impossible underestimation of the American colonies (p.112, 160) and the failure to actively advocate for the abolition of the slave trade, despite his opposition to slavery in principle (p.501). In his final assessment, Roberts describes George III as a worthy and noble king who was misunderstood and maligned because of his unwavering commitment to constitutional monarchy and social conventions (p.675–676). In all of this, Roberts paints a portrait of George III that is unashamedly sympathetic, yet also balanced by careful thinking.

Roberts' assessment of King George's rule is buttressed by an impressive depth of historical research. Browsing Roberts' bibliography reveals that he has clearly gone to great lengths to master both the primary and secondary literature relevant to this subject. Furthermore, Roberts displays an impressive knowledge of George's eighteenth-century, trans-Atlantic milieu. Equipped with such knowledge, he labors to transport his readers into that world, so that they may better understand George III in his own time and place in history. At the same time, since the Georgian years were particularly characterized by an immense amount of social and political activity, there are occasions when Roberts' narrative of these events gets bogged down in the details. Readers who do not have a working knowledge of the era might especially struggle on this point. Nevertheless, Roberts does an admirable job of constructing an engaging and fluid narrative of a vast and complex subject. With all of this in mind, it is hard to argue with his conclusions about the nobility of King George III. Despite the difficulties, this book deserves a wide reading, but it will prove especially useful to those who seek a better understanding of the social and political context of this period.

Finally, it is worth noting that *The Last King of America* will challenge many readers in their perception of King George III and the events surrounding the American Revolution—but this is all the more reason to read it. Not everyone will agree with Roberts' conclusions, and some American readers are likely to take offense at his description of the Declaration of Independence as "grotesquely hypocritical, illogical, mendacious, and sublime" (p.306). Others, however, will come away from this work with a completely new perspective on King George's life and reign, as well as the events which resulted in the American founding. This is precisely the kind of new perspective that Roberts seeks to bring with this book. Readers would be wise to welcome such a challenge to their preconceived notions with open arms.

Zachary Williams
PhD cand., The Southern Baptist Theological Seminary
Louisville, Kentucky

Ian Hugh Clary, *Reformed Evangelicalism and the Search for a Useable Past: The Historiography of Arnold Dallimore, Pastor-Historian*, Reformed Historical Theology (Göttingen: Vandenhoeck & Ruprecht, 2020), 266 pages.

The relationship between evangelicals and the writing of history can often appear to be a tangled web of competing visions and methodologies. Recent literature tends to take a sociological or political angle—and arrives at mostly negative conclusions. This literature has also been inclined to focus exclusively on evangelicals in the United States with someone like Billy Graham as the exemplar. Evangelicalism as a movement, however, is older and geographically broader than such a narrow scope. In this work, Ian Clary attempts to address some of the challenges that face evangelicals in the process of writing their own history through the story of the Canadian-British figure, Arnold Dallimore (1911–1998).

Clary serves as Assistant Professor of Historical Theology at Colorado Christian University, and this publication is a result of his doctoral dissertation supervised by Michael A.G. Haykin and Adriaan C. Neele. Though it is an academic monograph, it is quite accessible and well worth the price. One of Clary's goals is to adjudicate the charge often levied against Dallimore—namely, that he was guilty of hagiography. The early chapters engage with the nature of historiography, while the rest of the book is largely biographical. Clary additionally uses the life and work of Dallimore as a case study of a prominent evangelical pastor-historian.

Clary demonstrates clearly that Dallimore was a major figure in the revival of interest in Calvinistic Evangelicalism, particularly through his involvement with the Banner of Truth publishing house. Dallimore was widely known for his two-volume biography of George Whitefield and another on Charles Spurgeon, but he also wrote biographies of Edward Irving as well as Charles and Susannah Wesley. As indicated above, the real core of the book is an appraisal of *how* Dallimore told the stories of these Christian lives. In short, Clary concludes that Dallimore was *not* guilty of hagiography. He bases this on a number of considerations, including Dallimore's academic experience, vocational call, and intended audience. Dallimore's primary vocation was the pastorate, and thus he did not have the privilege of advanced training in history as a formal discipline. With his primary audience being the church, spiritual edification and encouragement (over and against a critical monograph) was his goal. The factors above do not map on to what is typically considered proper academic writing. Here the distinction between pastoral care and hagiographical intention is made—Clary argues that readers should judge Dallimore for what he was *trying* to do, instead of imparting a motivation that Dallimore would not recognize.

This book is an excellent work of scholarship, surveying substantial primary and secondary literature, private correspondence, unpublished manuscripts, and even including first-person interviews with Dallimore's widow, May Bredin Dallimore (1921–2015). These sources enable Clary to convey the inspiring perseverance of the Dallimores through long-term adversity: physical, financial, and emotional (p.105). Clary does not shy away from Dallimore's own weaknesses. For instance, he notes how Dallimore's anti-charismatic bent led him to a "theological agenda [that] clouded his historical judgment" of Edward Irving (p.238).

An eminently helpful section was Chapter 2, where Clary surveys the various debates and methods of Christian historiography. It is here that addresses the idea of the "usable past," which is "rooted in the idea that since the past shapes the present, it can be used to inform and guide the present" (p.17). A natural question arises as to how (or whether) a Christian should use the past. To answer this, Clary asks "Is there a Christian way to do history?" (p.24). Without reservation he answers in the affirmative—yet practitioners remain divided as to how to go about such a task. He surveys the last sixty years or so of Christian historical societies and institutions in order to explain the divide, exploring the Conference on Faith and History, the Christianity and History Forum, and the Evangelical History Association. Additionally, he summarizes the contributions of some leading scholars such as George Marsden, Mark Noll, David Bebbington, and Andrew Atherstone. Clary provides a general taxonomy by articulating the two extremities of the spectrum: the supernaturalist perspective at one end and the naturalist perspective at the other. It is between these worlds that Clary offers his own alternative mediating position.

Clary's middle path fittingly recognizes that the fundamental difference between the naturalist and supernaturalist has much to do with the intended audience of the work. Popular history will be written in a different style than that of academic history. And similarly, history for the church should be written in a different mode and with different emphases than history written for the academy. This is the precise case that Clary makes for Dallimore's value in the remainder of the book—Dallimore wrote non-academic biography for the church, and thus it should not be measured as if it were academic history for the historical guild.

Building on the work of others, Clary argues that the book of Esther is evidence that the Bible permits different approaches to religious people telling religious history. Esther is unique among the canonical books in that it never mentions the name of Yahweh, and yet the Jewish worldview saturates the book with Yahweh as the hero. In a similar way, a naturalist Christian historian may narrate his or her own history for the academy without centering (or overtly featuring) the direct intervention of God, and even refrain from making interpretations about God's providential purposes. Likewise, the supernaturalist

Christian historian can follow the pattern set by other biblical historical books like Moses, the Chronicler, and Luke in writing meaningful providential history for the church—as long as he or she is careful to avoid common pitfalls like hagiography or anachronism (57). Despite those who might dissent, Clary asserts that evangelicals may indeed operate by the methodological rules of the historical guild without conceding their religious beliefs.

This book is an excellent reflection on the historian's task, especially the historical biographer. It is a valuable contribution to the corpus of literature with its telling of the life and work of Arnold Dallimore and his place in the development of evangelical historiography. Anyone studying the art and science of biography, the worlds of Whitefield and Spurgeon, or the history of evangelicalism would benefit from this book. If the price is a deterrent, it would be worthwhile to reach out to your library and request for them to add it to their publications.

Garrett Walden
Pastor, Grace Heritage Church, Auburn, Alabama

Dallas W. Vandiver, *Who Can Take the Lord's Supper: A Biblical-Theological Argument for Close Communion* (Eugene, OR: Pickwick Publications, 2021), 387 pages.

The question posed by the title of this book has vexed Baptists, especially Calvinistic Baptists, over the centuries. William Kiffen and John Bunyan debated it in the late seventeenth century; Abraham Booth and Robert Robinson discussed it towards the end of the eighteenth century and Andrew Fuller also wrote on the subject; in the early nineteenth century, Robert Hall and Joseph Kinghorn engaged in an extended exchange of treatises over the issue. Others, on both sides of the Atlantic, have weighed in on the controversy from one perspective or another. Confessionally, the Second London Confession of Faith maintains a studious silence on the question, deliberately allowing both open and closed communionists to subscribe. Nevertheless, the debate is an important one. And those who hold to a Baptistic Reformed theology, particularly ministers and elders, need to know what they believe, given the very practical implications of the question: who, indeed, can take the Lord's Supper?

Dallas Vandiver has performed a valuable service in the research, preparation and production of this volume, which began life as his PhD dissertation at The Southern Baptist Theological Seminary. He rightly notes that the historical debates on this topic among Baptists have tended to neglect its biblical-theological perspective. The arguments have focused on New Testament teaching and church practice and have made relatively little reference to the Old Testament, though both sides of the debate have made use of the express injunction in Exodus 12:48 that forbids the uncircumcised from participating in the Passover. Vandiver has therefore set out to supply an in-depth analysis of the biblical-theological principles that govern the relationship between the various covenant signs of Old and New Testaments: between circumcision and Passover, between baptism and the Lord's Supper and, finally, between old covenant and new covenant signs. The covenantal approach that Vandiver favours for this exercise is, he says, the 'progressive covenantal' approach advocated by Peter J. Gentry and Stephen J. Wellum in their *Kingdom through Covenant* (Wheaton, IL: Crossway, 2012).

The book categorises the various views on participation in the Lord's Supper into four. The view for which the author argues is denoted 'close communion' and permits participation in the Lord's Supper by those who have been baptised by immersion on profession of faith and who are members in good standing of the church administering the ordinance or of a church of like faith and practice. This is contrasted with 'open communion', where the Table is open to all professing believers in Christ, regardless of how or even whether they have been baptised: the basis of participation in the Lord's Supper for the open communionist, on this definition, is regeneration rather than baptism. 'Closed communion' is where the Table is open only to members of the administering local church, baptised by immersion on profession of their faith. Vandiver's fourth category is what he terms 'ecumenical communion', according to which the Lord's Table is open to anyone who has undergone any form of baptism, or even, where baptism is regarded as a converting ordinance, to those who have not been baptised at all.

In its opening chapter, the book reviews the historical controversies on this issue. The various arguments are well summarised, briefly but helpfully. They demonstrate the justification for the book by showing that its main focus, concerning the move from Old to New Testament covenant signs and the connection between them, has not been argued in detail in the historical debates on the subject. The substantive exposition of the book's thesis begins in Chapter 2, which examines the Old Testament covenant signs. It contains a detailed, though summary, discussion of the significance of circumcision, concluding that, among other things, it pointed typologically to the circumcision of the heart. Circumcision was a prerequisite to participation in the Passover, which was a covenantal meal that 'inaugurated the saving events of the exodus by which God brought Israel into covenant relationship with himself' and 'served as a yearly covenantal celebration and memorial for Israel's redemption'. It related also to the covenant ratification meal at Sinai.

The new covenant signs of baptism and the Lord's Supper and their inter-relationship are considered in Chapter 3. Believers are to be baptised and this, on the New Testament evidence, precedes participation in the Lord's Supper. Baptism is the covenantal entry sign and the Lord's Supper the sign of ongoing covenantal participation. The participants in the Lord's Supper are those who are united by faith to Christ, externally appropriated by baptism. The Lord's Supper is an 'ongoing sign of participation in the new covenant'; it functions as a 'new covenant ratification meal and a proleptic kingdom feast in anticipation of the Marriage Supper of the Lamb' (p.168).

Vandiver examines in Chapter 4 the connections between old and new covenant signs. His argument is that 'the continuities and discontinuities between the covenant signs reveal that the new covenant signs are analogically similar to a sufficient degree to the old covenant signs to suggest that baptism should precede communion' (p.205–206). Circumcision and baptism both 'function as boundary markers and initiating oath signs (or signs of entry) into God's covenant people' and 'entail heart circumcision' (prospectively in circumcision, reflectively in baptism) (p.206). Each sign 'marks off a distinct "political institution" through which God intends to display his character to the world and bless the nations' (p.207). The Lord's Supper is the inaugurated fulfillment of Passover. Both meals are acts of remembrance, emblematic of God's reign over his enemies and the deliverance of his people from them. They are anticipatory of the arrival of God's kingdom and covenantal presence.

Alongside these continuities, Vandiver lists a significant number of discontinuities between circumcision and baptism and between Passover and the Lord's Supper. There are differences in, among other things, the subjects of the signs, the need for faith, the nature of the covenant communities to which they relate and the divine promises and events that accompany them. Accounting for the various continuities and discontinuities that he has identified, Vandiver points to Christ as the typological seed of Abraham, the seed to whom all the Abrahamic promises were intended and the one with whom the new covenant is made. Christ's fulfilment of the covenant 'grounds not only the shift of covenant signs but also the shift in the nature and structure of the covenant community' (p. 241).

On the basis of this biblical-theological analysis, Vandiver concludes that it is legitimate to argue from the Old Testament prohibition of the uncircumcised's participating in Passover to a New Testament requirement that baptism precede participation in the Lord's Supper. This ineluctably leads to the conclusion that Baptist churches should practise close communion. Vandiver argues this out in detail in Chapter 5, showing in Chapter 6 how the New Testament locates the Lord's Supper firmly within the context of the local church and setting out practical implications connected with the administration of the Supper in that context.

This volume contains a great deal of detailed exegesis and theological argument on a range of topics that are connected to the main thesis. Not all of this material is strictly necessary to that thesis, though it is all of some degree of relevance to it. This no doubt reflects the book's origin as a PhD dissertation. It makes the book a very useful resource indeed for anyone interested in researching aspects of the Baptist communion controversies—references to primary and secondary material will readily be found. It has the disadvantage, however, of threatening to mask the main argument of the book and dull the force of its central thesis. More than once, the reader may wonder what precisely some of the detail adds to that thesis. Those who favour open (or ecumenical) communion might question whether the wealth of information that Vandiver presents on the relationship between old and new covenant signs clearly demonstrates that the continuities between them outweigh the discontinuities, such that the strictness of order as between the Old Testament signs must be replicated in the New. Even so, the book supplies a very persuasive addition to the arguments for close communion marshalled by Booth, Fuller, Kinghorn and others in the historical debates and will prove very useful as a resource for all who wish to explore in depth the biblical-theological relationships between the covenant signs of the Old and New Testaments.

Robert Strivens
Pastor, Bradford on Avon Baptist Church

William H. Brackney, and Evan L. Colford, eds., *Come Out from among Them, and Be Ye Separate, Saith the Lord: Separationism and the Believers' Church Tradition* (Eugene, OR: Pickwick Publications, 2019), xix + 235 pages.

Representing the proceedings of the 17th Believers' Church Conference held in 2016 at Acadia Divinity College, Brackney and Colford's volume provides "the first examination of the phenomenon [of separationism] among the Believers' Churches and it should become an authority in this generation" (p. xiv). Besides mainly historical studies on the causes and types of separation within or across specific Believers' Church traditions (BCTs), most chapters provide theological reflection aiming to mitigate future divisions in churches of the BCT. Overall, the conference proceedings lack careful editing, and some of the included calls to unity are unfeasible, but numerous excellent contributions preserve the worth of the volume and merit study for those researching separationism, especially in the BCT.

The book is divided into three parts. Part I includes chapters on why Christians from 1400 to 1600 were led to form new churches (Martin Rothkegel, ch. 1); typological factors inciting impulsive separationism among Baptists (William Brackney, ch. 2); how Anabaptists' credobaptism and imminent eschatology fueled their early divisions and mission (Colin Godwin, ch. 3); the Stone-Campbell Restoration Movement's initial call to primitive unity that eventually splintered into multiple denominations (Douglas Foster, ch. 4); and why Mennonites should adopt the metaphor of a rhizome for navigating LGBTQ+ divisions and other controversies (John Roth, ch. 5). Part II features chapters on the pietist devotion of British Baptist women during the 17th and 18th centuries (Karen Smith, ch. 6); how members of North American black Baptist churches have necessarily separated to secure opportunities for ministry (David Goatley, ch. 7); why Baptists and Disciples of Christ in Canada's Maritime Provinces formed fraternal bonds rather than merging during 1903–1908 (Russell Prime, ch. 8); and how Pentecostalism in Newfoundland grew out of decaying Methodism in the 20th century, yet unconsciously retrieved much of Methodism's early character (Allison MacGregor, ch. 9). Part III contains a chapter on trends—not generalizations—of new religious movements (NRMs) and characteristic reactions to them since the 20th century (Eileen Barker, ch. 10), and another that formulates a vision for what should unite members of the BCT, especially for ecumenical dialogue (Teun van der Leer, ch. 11).

Editorially, the book has dozens of typos, including every chapter and section but the preface. The front cover says the book was edited by Brackney "with" Colford, while the copyright page says "and" (p.v). The first BCT conference began in 1967 but the back cover says during "the late 1950s" (cf. ch. 11 and p.200). Numerous chapters left traces of the original oral delivery, such as Brackney ("So, there is a strange pride of place in this Believers' Church Conference that Baptists should present first," p.24, although ch. 2) and Roth ("During the past year, three regional conferences and numerous individual congregations—more than 600 congregations altogether—have formally left MCUSA, with others either contemplating a departure or actively seeking new forms of relating to the denomination" p.71, referring to the conference rather than publication year; cf. also pp. 4, 34, 197). Most disconcerting was the editors' choice—which James M. Stayer critiques in the foreword (p.x–xi)—to include Barker's chapter on non-Christian NRMs in a book on separationism in the BCT. Despite Baker's attempt to maintain impartiality as a secular sociologist (she is obviously an expert in her field), her labeling Mormons as a (Christian) church and Plymouth Brethren as a sect belies her supposed neutrality (p.158–60, 167, 170, 181; cf. 179). Without any disrespect to Barker's insightful article, its inclusion reduces the book's cohesion. One wonders why another representative of the BCT (e.g., Plymouth Brethren) did not find a place instead.

Concerning unfeasible calls to action, the contributions of Roth and van der Leer warrant a response. Roth pleads for Mennonites not to continue separating over issues of sexuality, preferring them to remain united and view themselves as a rhizome, despite their differences. Given how the numerical—not the influential—center of gravity has shifted to the global south, Roth asks, "What sort of transformation of mind and heart—what kind of renewal—might such a ["rhizomic"] vision require of those 7 percent of Mennonites in North America who are used to thinking of ourselves as being at the center of the church, rather than the periphery?" (p.77) His question seems purely rhetorical. Were the MCUSA and MC Canada, for example, to implement such listening to the global south, they would likely find themselves in a position analogous to the United Methodist Church in 2019. Thus, instead of following through on his rhetoric, Roth defaults to old calls for patience (p.81–82) and leaning on the Spirit's guiding (p.77, 82), as though somehow Scripture is unclear on these matters.

Finding fault with earlier definitions of the BCT, van der Leer offers a vision of its being what we might call *congregationalist, credobaptist, covenanted/committed*, and *ante-creedal* (my term; p.194–197). The congregationalist criterion is problematic since many Anabaptist churches have historically been episcopalian. Most problematic is what I term ante-creedal, or what another whom he quotes approvingly calls "'belonging before believing'" (p.197; see p.194–196 and cf. p.20–21), One might say that van der Leer's vision fits rather a *Belongers'* Church. It is reminiscent of Foster's descriptions of the Restoration Movement with its calls to "unite" (though substitute "belong") eventually resulting in more divisions.

Overall, the editors gathered a solid array of scholars to instantiate separation for a wide array of reasons within the BCT. The historical examples merit careful reflection over the causes for separation, helping one to appreciate why the notion of *theological triage* (coined by Albert Mohler) has become so valued. Those whose traditions are analyzed here would do well to think carefully over the assessed reasons for separation. One can only hope that the book will facilitate unity within—and beyond—the BCT where able and, where not, that God's call to separate will continue to be heeded.

Kyle Young
Pastor, Bluesky Christian Fellowship
(affiliated with the Northwest Mennonite Conference)
Bluesky, Alberta

CENTER *for* BAPTIST STUDIES
at THE SOUTHERN BAPTIST THEOLOGICAL SEMINARY

The Andrew Fuller Center for Baptist Studies, located at The Southern Baptist Theological Seminary in Louisville, Kentucky, seeks to promote the study of Baptist history as well as theological reflection on the contemporary significance of that history. The center is named in honor of Andrew Fuller (1754–1815), the late eighteenth- and early nineteenth- century English Baptist pastor and theologian, who played a key role in opposing aberrant thought in his day as well as being instrumental in the founding and early years of the Baptist Missionary Society. Fuller was a close friend and theological mentor of William Carey, one of the pioneers of that society.

The Andrew Fuller Center holds an annual two-day conference in September that examines various aspects of Baptist history and thought. It also supports the publication of the critical edition of the Works of Andrew Fuller, and from time to time, other works in Baptist history. The Center seeks to play a role in the mentoring of junior scholars interested in studying Baptist history.

andrewfullercenter.org

DE GRUYTER

The Andrew Fuller Works Project
It is with deep gratitude to God that The Andrew Fuller Center for Baptist Studies announces that the publishing house of Walter de Gruyter, with head offices in Berlin and Boston, has committed itself to the publication of a modern critical edition of the entire corpus of Andrew Fuller's published and unpublished works. Walter de Gruyter has been synonymous with high-quality, landmark publications in both the humanities and sciences for more than 260 years. The preparation of a critical edition of Fuller's works, part of the work of the Andrew Fuller Center, was first envisioned in 2004. It is expected that this edition this edition will comprise seventeen volumes.

The importance of the project
The controlling objective of The Works of Andrew Fuller Project is to preserve and accurately transmit the text of Fuller's writings. The editors are committed to the finest scholarly standards for textual transcription, editing, and annotation. Transmitting these texts is a vital task since Fuller's writings, not only for their volume, extent, and scope, but for their enduring importance, are major documents in both the Baptist story and the larger history of British Dissent.

From a merely human perspective, if Fuller's theological works had not been written, William Carey would not have gone to India. Fuller's theology was the mainspring behind the formation and early development of the Baptist Missionary Society, the first foreign missionary society created by the Evangelical Revival of the last half of the eighteenth century and the missionary society under whose auspices Carey went to India. Very soon, other missionary societies were established, and a new era in missions had begun as the Christian faith was increasingly spread outside of the West, to the regions of Africa and Asia. Carey was most visible at the fountainhead of this movement. Fuller, though not so visible, was utterly vital to its genesis.

andrewfullercenter.org/the-andrew-fuller-works-project

H&E Publishing is a Canadian evangelical publishing company located out of Peterborough, Ontario. We exist to provide Christ-exalting, Gospel-centred, and Bible-saturated content aimed to show God to be as glorious and worthy as He truly is.

hesedandemet.com